TERRORIST GROUP PROFILES

Fredonia Books
Amsterdam, The Netherlands

Terrorist Group Profiles

By
The Vice President´s Task Force on Combatting Terrorism
Introduction by George Bush
Preface by Frank C. Carlucci, III

ISBN: 1-58963-709-7

Copyright © 2002 by Fredonia Books

Reprinted from the original edition

Fredonia Books
Amsterdam, the Netherlands
http://www.fredoniabooks.com

Fellow Americans: November 1988

In February 1986, The Vice President's Task Force on Combatting Terrorism released its public report, which contained a number of policy recommendations. These recommendations became the cornerstone of US counterterrorism policy. One key proposal was to launch a public awareness effort to better inform the American people about the nature of terrorism and the threat it represents to our national security interests and to the freedoms we so deeply cherish.

I strongly favor providing the public such information because it sharpens awareness as to the individual agendas of terrorist groups, the role of nations that support their depredations, and the necessity for tailoring multiple strategies to effectively combat this scourge.

As a result of the findings of my Task Force, we have markedly improved the coordinating machinery that enables the American Government to more rapidly and effectively resolve terrorist crises. We have put in place new procedures to enhance the response capabilities of our intelligence, law enforcement, and security forces. We have spent millions to recruit, train, and equip our personnel engaged in combatting terrorism and to enhance the security of our embassies and overseas military bases.

My Task Force outlined a clear and concise counterterrorism policy — the toughest in the Free World.

First, the United States will be firm with terrorists. We will not make concessions. We will continue to urge other countries not to make concessions. Rewarding terrorists only encourages more terrorism. Second, we will apply pressure to states which sponsor terrorism. We will work with friendly nations to apply diplomatic, economic, political, and, if necessary, military pressure on states which sponsor terrorism. If we find states supplying money, weapons, training, identification documents, travel, or safehaven for terrorists, we will respond. Our aim is to demonstrate to these countries that supporting terrorism is not cost-free.

Third, we will bring terrorists to justice. We will continue to cooperate with friendly nations to identify, track, apprehend, prosecute, and punish terrorists. Our efforts include exchanging intelligence information on terrorists and their movements, developing "watch lists" for use by border police, and tightening extradition treaties. Terrorism is crime, and terrorists must be treated as criminals.

In addition, the United States will help friendly nations resist terrorist pressures through an ambitious program of antiterrorism training which, since 1984, has trained more than 6,000 police officers and security personnel from some 50 nations.

Our policy has been effective. From 1986-1987, the number of anti-US terrorist attacks dropped 25 percent. International terrorist operations in Western Europe over the past 2 years decreased 31 percent, and last year in Latin America dropped 32 percent. Only two international terrorist skyjackings occurred in 1986 and only one in 1987. Particularly gratifying have been the increasingly successful prosecutions of international terrorists. Last year alone, there were 30 convictions in 9 different countries — the majority of terrorists received sentences of death, or life imprisonment.

Although progress has been made, terrorism remains a serious threat. In 1987, international terrorists carried out 832 operations, attacking the citizens and property of 84 nations. More than 2,000 persons were wounded. More than 600 died. This was greater than any year since the US Government began keeping records some 20 years ago.

The surge in the level of international terrorist activity worldwide in 1987 and 1988 resulted from a wave of high-casualty bombings in Pakistan carried out by agents of the Afghan intelligence service known as WAD. The WAD is Soviet trained and organized. The terrorist campaign is designed to deter the Government of Pakistan from aiding resistance fighters in Afghanistan. Fully one-third of all deaths and one-half of all injuries in 1987 that resulted worldwide from international terrorist operations were attributable to this campaign of terror — a campaign that left in its wake more than 220 dead and 1,000 wounded. When these numbers are subtracted, the number of incidents in the rest of the world declined by almost 10 percent from the 1986 statistics.

Many other states have adopted terrorism as a tool of foreign policy. Incidents attributable to state sponsorship rose from 70 attacks in 1986 to 189 in 1987, an increase of more than 170 percent. Governments sponsoring terrorism include North Korea, Iran, Libya, Syria, and South Yemen. This past year, only Syria took steps to lessen its support of terrorism by expelling the Abu Nidal Organization from the country.

For many, terrorism represents a cheap and effective way to project power. It is a tactic that enables terrorists to shoot their way onto the world stage and, in effect, hijack the international media. Terrorism, as common street crime, may never be totally eradicated, but we can reduce it to a more tolerable level. In our fight against terrorism we are going to suffer casualties. And, as in any conflict, the innocent suffer. Our aim is to minimize the price the American people and other innocents pay, and assure that those states and groups that resort to terrorism find the cost prohibitive and their actions counterproductive.

The difference between terrorists and freedom fighters is sometimes clouded. Some would say one man's freedom fighter is another man's terrorist. I reject this notion. The philosophical differences are stark and fundamental. It should be clear to all those who read this book that terrorists are criminals who attack our cherished institutions and profane our values.

In seeking to destroy freedom and democracy, terrorists deliberately target noncombatants for their own cynical purposes. They kill and maim defenseless men, women, and children. They murder judges, newspaper reporters, elected officials, government administrators, labor leaders, policemen, priests, and others who defend the values of civilized society. Freedom fighters, in contrast, seek to adhere to international law and civilized standards of conduct. They attack military targets, not defenseless civilians. Noncombatant casualties in this context are an aberration or attributable to the fortunes of war. They are not the result of deliberate policy designed to terrorize the opposition.

The difference between the terrorists and the freedom fighters is as profound as it is obvious. To permit this distinction to become blurred is to play into terrorists' hands.

The American public needs to understand terrorism, what it is and is not, and how the United States Government takes action against the terrorist threat.

Sincerely,

George Bush

Preface

International terrorism has become an increasing challenge to the international rule of law and a major concern of the United States Government. In order to combat terrorism effectively, it is necessary to know the enemy. International terrorism is not a monolithic phenomenon. Terrorist groups differ significantly in terms of their aims, strategies, organization, capabilities, and a host of other attributes. They represent many disparate and often antagonistic causes, and they cover the ideological spectrum.

The United States represents a prime target for terrorist groups because of our commitment to political reform and constructive change. To terrorists, reform is anathema, for it represents continuation of the system they abhor and co-opts the revolution they hope to lead.

Terrorism is essentially a tactic — a form of political warfare designed to achieve political ends. It falls under the rubric of low-intensity conflict, which may be described as warfare at the lower end of the spectrum of violence, in which political, economic, and psychosocial considerations play a more important role than does conventional military power.

US Government representatives abroad have become prime terrorist targets. Captain "Bill" Nordeen, USN, our Defense Attache in Athens, was the most recent US fatality. He was murdered by assassins from the 17 November Organization only days before he was to return to the US and begin his well-deserved retirement. American businessmen, tourists, diplomats, military personnel, students, and even missionaries have become terrorist victims. The aim of such attacks is to discourage a US presence abroad, reduce our investments in overseas markets, and thereby erode US influence as a global power.

Within the target country, the terrorists' objective is to undermine confidence in the ability of the national government to provide basic security. The aim is to create economic and political dislocation that will ultimately render the target government incapable of governing. In such situations, a power vacuum is created which those challenging the government attempt to fill.

The study that follows is designed to provide the American people detailed information about key terrorist groups and thereby strip away much of their mystique. We anticipate it will be useful to researchers, students, the media, and others who follow terrorist issues. The study is divided into geographic sections that begin with an overview, followed by coverage of the key regional terrorist groups. Information includes an estimate of each group's membership strength, identities of key leaders, ideological orientation, target audiences, a narrative description of the group's background, and a selected incident chronology.

By providing such detailed information, we can help the American people understand better the terrorist phenomenon and place it in perspective as one of many challenges we must confront in this complex and sometimes violent age.

Frank C. Carlucci, III
Secretary of Defense

Table of Contents

Table of Contents (Continued)

Experts use a wide variety of definitions to describe the phenomenon of terrorism, but no single one has gained universal acceptance. For recording and coding data on terrorist incidents, this study adheres to definitions that represent a middle ground within the broad range of expert opinion, both foreign and domestic.

Terrorism is premeditated, politically motivated violence perpetrated against noncombatant targets by subnational groups or clandestine state agents, usually to influence an audience.

International terrorism is terrorism involving citizens or territory of more than one country.

Introduction

On any single day, acts of terrorism take place around the world for a variety of motives. Whether the terrorists style themselves as separatists, anarchists, dissidents, nationalists, Marxist revolutionaries, or religious true believers, what marks them as terrorists is that they direct their violence against noncombatants with the goal of terrorizing a wider audience than the immediate victims, thereby attempting to gain political influence over the larger audience.

On a theoretical plane, it is possible to discern several variants of terrorism among its practitioners; although these variants have distinctive characteristics, they also frequently overlap.

One such variant is organizational terrorism. Mostly small, tightly knit, and politically homogeneous, such groups are incapable of developing popular support for their radical positions and therefore resort to terrorism to gain influence. Examples include the Red Army Faction and the Revolutionary Cells in West Germany, the Red Brigades in Italy, Direct Action in France, and 17 November in Greece. Others of this general type have become transnational in their terrorist reach — having the potential to conduct terrorism almost anywhere in the world. The most notorious example of a transnational terrorist group that is basically of the organizational variant is the Abu Nidal Organization, a radical Palestinian group that has targeted civilians indiscriminately in its terrorist operations in many different countries. Others include the Japanese Red Army, whose recent reemergence on the terrorist scene is of deep concern, and the Armenian Secret Army for the Liberation of Armenia, which has been relatively inactive of late.

Another variant of terrorism is conducted within the context of insurgencies. Insurgencies can be ethnic separatist or country-wide. Normally they are wide-scale revolts against the established government conducted by paramilitary or guerrilla forces operating within the boundaries of the state under seige. These insurgent forces, however, frequently have a terrorist component seeking to undermine the government's credibility, legitimacy, and public support by directing terror at civilians.

An example is the New People's Army, the military wing of the Communist Party of the Philippines; in addition to insurgent activity, the New People's Army conducts terror to demonstrate that the Philippine Government cannot protect its people. Equally troublesome are terrorist acts undertaken to prove the continuing vitality of an insurgent group when its battlefield fortunes are declining, as seen in El Salvador and Colombia in the recent past.

A third variant — the one that poses the greatest challenge to the United States and other freedom-loving countries — is state-sponsored terrorism. This is direct sponsorship or abetment of terrorist groups and their actions by sovereign states. Such state sponsorship makes this terrorism deadlier, lengthens the reach of the terrorist activities, and is a matter of growing international concern.

Iran, Afghanistan, and Libya are among the most notorious state sponsors of terrorism. Syria was previously in this rank; however, following revelations in European courts of its involvement in terrorist acts in 1985-86, international pressure forced it to appear to mend its ways. By its blatantly terroristic act in November 1987 of downing a civilian South Korean airliner, North Korea clearly marked itself as a terrorist state sponsor. State sponsorship can take place at varied levels:

- Conducting actual terrorist operations (as did North Korea in destroying the South Korean airliner and Afghanistan in sending its agents into Pakistan to conduct an extensive bombing campaign).
- Providing encouragement, direction, and material assistance to terrorist groups

conducting their own attacks, which are also in the sponsoring state's interest (as Iran and Libya frequently have done by operating through terrorist surrogates). Providing weapons, explosives, training, safe passage, safehaven, and ideological justification (as do the state sponsors already mentioned, as well as South Yemen and others, to include some of the Soviet Bloc countries).

These states sponsor terrorism for varying reasons. Some do so to complement other instruments of state policy — to achieve foreign policy objectives that could not otherwise be achieved through conventional political or military means. Some states sponsor terrorism to create or expand their power and influence among ideological or religious movements, or as a means of establishing credentials with revolutionary movements worldwide. Still other state-sponsored terrorist incidents are geared

at stifling domestic opposition through selective assassination of dissidents abroad.

For the most part, state sponsors of terrorism attempt to hide their involvement through proxies and other means. Their actions frequently are difficult to trace, so that they can maintain respectability and legitimacy in the world community while covertly sponsoring subversion and terror to achieve their goals.

This publication is designed to be a useful reference for those within and outside the government who study international terrorism, whether as security specialists, reporters, academics, or policy planners. The report profiles the more notorious terrorists groups, providing overviews of their political objectives, backgrounds, target audiences, and sponsors, plus a select chronology of their acts through 1987.

International Incidents

Number of Incidents

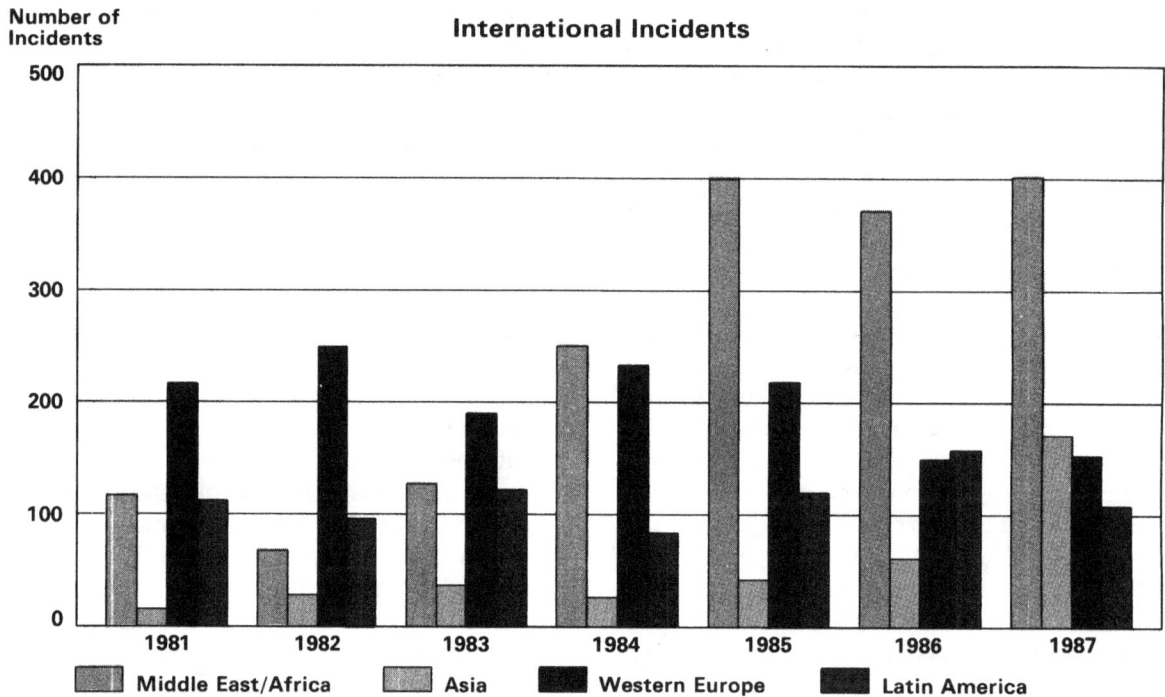

Middle East/Africa   Asia   Western Europe   Latin America

Middle Eastern Terrorism

Middle Eastern terrorism revolves around the issues of a Palestinian homeland, Israel's existence and policies, Arab states jockeying for regional power, sectarian strife, religious extremism, and, until recently, the Iran-Iraq War. The dramatic rise of Middle Eastern terrorism is a direct result of the steady growth of state support. Middle East groups and state agents have operated globally and have obtained sophisticated arms, extensive logistics, precise intelligence, and safehaven.

This region's most notorious practitioner of terrorism, Libyan military dictator Colonel Muammar Al-Qadhafi, historically has employed terrorism to lash out against regime opponents and to further his own foreign policy objectives within the Arab political arena and within worldwide revolutionary movements. Libyan People's Bureaus abroad, Revolutionary Committees, the Anti-Imperialism Center in Tripoli, numerous front organizations, and intelligence and security services all have been called upon at times to support Libyan terrorism. Following the April 1986 US airstrikes, however, detectable Libyan involvement in terrorist activity dropped significantly through 1987. Nevertheless, Qadhafi shows no sign of forsaking terrorism, and Libyan agents continue to track and kill opponents of the regime. Qadhafi has turned increasingly to surrogates for attacks, seeking greater plausible denial and safety from retaliation. Libya now hosts the most extreme Palestinian terrorist group — the Abu Nidal Organization — and there are other signs that Libyan involvement in terrorism may be again on the rise.

Syria, under President Assad, previously was an active, if not a more calculated, sponsor of terrorism. Syrian operations normally were confined to the Middle East, although Western Europe occasionally has been the venue for its activities. Three acts of Syrian terrorism occurred in Europe in 1986: an attempted bombing of the El Al airline in London, the bombing of the German-Arab friendship society in Berlin, and the bombing of the El Al ticket counter in Madrid. These attacks drew intense international criticism and sanctions, forcing Syria to distance itself from its previously close association with terrorism, although more circumspect support for terrorist acts in the Middle East likely will continue.

The Khomeini regime in Iran views terrorism as a basic tactic to be used against US and other Western influence and presence in the Middle East as well as a tool to foment Islamic fundamentalist revolution. Iran also uses terrorism to intimidate Arab states in the Persian Gulf and as another means to wage war against Iraq and its allies.

Iran's principal surrogate, the Hizballah movement in Lebanon, has carried out car bombings, kidnapings, hijackings, and other acts of terrorism against Western interests since 1983. Like Libya, and previously Syria, Iran uses its government apparatus to recruit, train, finance, and deploy terrorists, especially in Lebanon.

Among the most longstanding and well-known practitioners of terrorism in the Middle East and elsewhere are the various Palestinian organizations that emerged in the 1960s and the 1970s. The best known Palestinian organization is the Palestine Liberation Organization (PLO), which was founded in 1964 as a nationalist umbrella organization dedicated to establishment of an independent Palestinian state. After the 1967 Arab-Israeli War, control over the PLO devolved to the leadership of the various *fedayeen* militia groups, the most dominant of which was the Fatah, led by Yasir Arafat. In 1969, Arafat became chairman of the PLO's Executive Committee, a position he still holds. The United States considers the PLO to be an umbrella organization that includes a number of differing constituent groups and individuals who hold differing and often opposing views on terrorism. At the same time, US policy has taken into account that elements of the PLO have actively advocated, carried out, or accepted responsibility for acts of terrorism.

In the early 1970s, several PLO groups, including the Fatah, carried out numerous international terrorist attacks. In the mid-1970s, under international pressure, the PLO claimed it would restrict its attacks to Israel and the occupied territories. Nonetheless, several terrorist attacks have been carried out since then by Fatah-affiliated groups (including the Hawari group and Force 17) and a PLO-affiliated group (the Palestine Liberation Front).

The most wide-ranging and vicious Palestinian terrorist group is the Abu Nidal Organization, which has killed scores of people in locations ranging from Karachi and Istanbul to Rome and Vienna. Other international terrorist groups include the Popular Front for the Liberation of Palestine — General Command, the Arab Organization of 15 May, and the Lebanese Armed Revolutionary Faction, a pro-Palestinian Lebanese terrorist group that has conducted its terrorist operations primarily in Western Europe.

Number of Incidents

Middle East Incidents

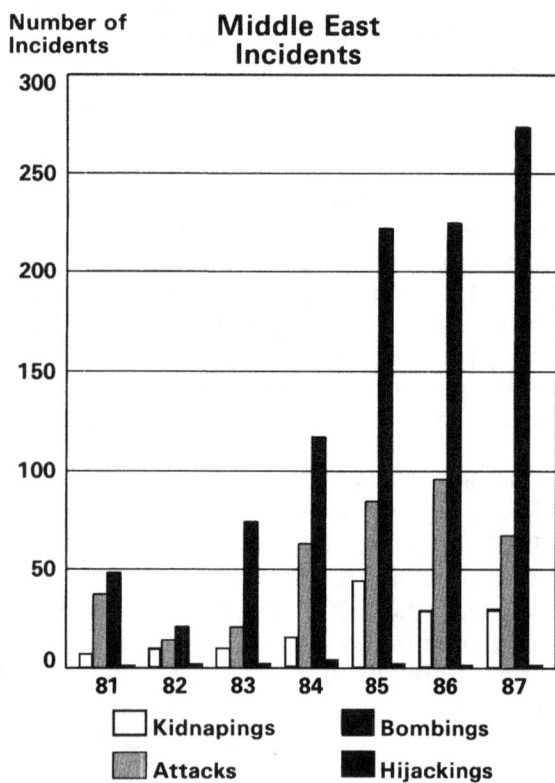

Kidnapings   Bombings
Attacks   Hijackings

Number of Incidents

Anti-US Attacks Middle East

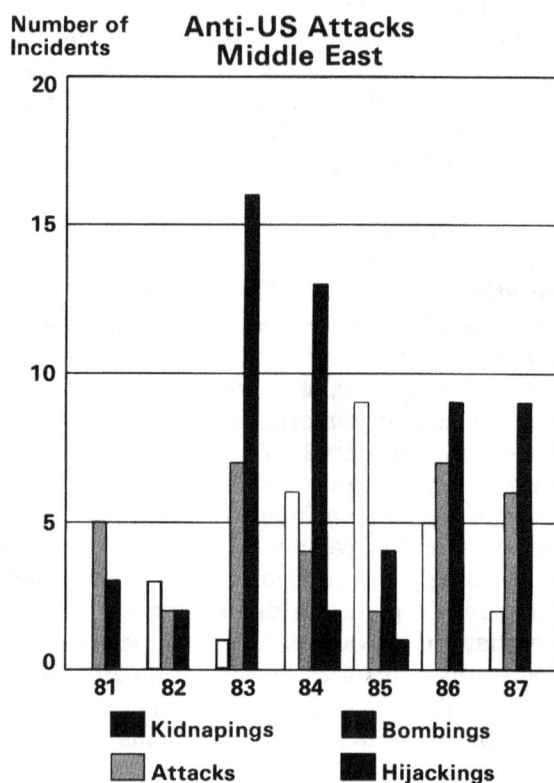

Kidnapings   Bombings
Attacks   Hijackings

Abu Nidal Organization (ANO)

Date Formed 1974.

Estimated Membership 500.

Headquarters Libya (previously Syria and Iraq).

Area of Operations International.

Leadership Sabri Khalil al-Banna (Abu Nidal).

Other Names Fatah — the Revolutionary Council (FRC), Black June Organization (BJO), Arab Revolutionary Brigades (ARB), Revolutionary Organization of Socialist Muslims (ROSM), Black September Organization (BSO).

Sponsors Previously Syria and Iraq, currently Libya; also self-sustaining economic operations.

Leader Sabri al-Banna a few years ago.

Political Objectives/Target Audiences
- Place the "armed struggle" against the "Zionist enemy" as the first priority of the Palestine resistance movement.
- Undermine efforts to negotiate an Israeli-Palestinian peace by terrorizing pro-Arafat Palestinians and by attacking Israeli targets in Europe and the Middle East.
- Threaten or attack "reactionary" regimes in Egypt, Jordan, Kuwait, Saudi Arabia, and the Gulf shaykhdoms.
- Affirm Arab commitment to the destruction of Israel.
- Intimidate those nations currently holding Abu Nidal operatives in prison into releasing them.

Background

A rejectionist and extremely violent Palestinian terrorist group, the Abu Nidal Organization opposes all efforts toward political reconciliation of the Arab-Israeli conflict. The group contends that both inter-Arab and intra-Palestinian terrorism are needed to precipitate an all-embracing Arab revolution that alone can lead to the liberation of occupied Palestine.

The Abu Nidal Organization is the most dangerous terrorist organization in existence, and its area of operations is one of the most extensive. The group made its initial appearance after the October 1973 Arab-Israeli War when Yasir Arafat decided to restrict terrorism only against Israeli targets in Israel and the occupied territories. Abu Nidal decided to fight any effort at moderation by continuing international terrorist operations against Israeli interests and by targeting pro-Arafat Palestinians and moderate Arab states. In fact, the rift between Abu Nidal and Arafat is so intense that Abu Nidal actually was sentenced to death, in absentia, by Arafat. Since 1973, the Abu Nidal Organization also has targeted those countries — primarily in Europe — that hold imprisoned operatives.

As Abu Nidal's following grew, the group's operations against Palestinian moderates escalated. In April 1978, 130 guerrillas were arrested with Fatah leader Muhammad Da'ud Awdah (Abu Da'ud),

5

who was preparing to disobey Arafat's orders and launch operations behind Israeli lines in southern Lebanon. These guerrillas are believed to have been sent by Abu Nidal, seeking to strengthen Fatah leftists and enable them to wrest control of Fatah from Arafat. During the first half of 1978, the Abu Nidal Organization assassinated three prominent PLO officials, who were allies of Arafat. Although a temporary rapprochement took place in 1978, the Abu Nidal Organization continues to target moderate Palestinian elements.

Despite its support by a succession of state sponsors (first Iraq, then Syria, and more recently Libya), the group maintains its own political agenda. Although many of the group's operations coincide with the interests of its state sponsors, the Abu Nidal organization also conducts independent operations.

Although rumors about the poor health — and even the demise — of Sabri Khalil al-Banna (Abu Nidal) abound, it is doubtful that his existence is essential to the organization's viability.

The Abu Nidal Organization is financially sound and may be one of the most economically viable of all terrorist organizations. The group is believed to draw one-third of its income from patron states, one-third from graft or blackmail, and one-third from its own network of business companies and front organizations.

Selected Incident Chronology

July 1980 — Claimed responsibility for killing the Israeli Commercial Attache in Brussels.

May 1981 — Murdered Viennese City Councilman Heinz Nittel and threatened to kill Austrian Chancellor Bruno Kreisky.

August 1981 — Machinegunned a Vienna synagogue, killing 2 and wounding 17.

June 1982 — Attempted assassination of Israeli Ambassador Shlomo Argov in London.

June 1982 — Killed PLO official Husayn Kamal in Rome with a car bomb.

August 1982 — Killed 6 and wounded 22 in a grenade and machinegun attack on a Parisian restaurant frequented by French Jews.

August 1982 — Attempted to murder the United Arab Emirates (UAE) Consul in Bombay.

August 1982 — Shot and wounded a UAE diplomat in his office in Kuwait.

September 1982 — Assassinated a Kuwaiti diplomat in Madrid.

October 1982 — Killed 1 child and injured 10 people in a grenade and machinegun attack on a Rome synagogue.

April 1983 — Murdered PLO official Issam Sartawi at the Socialist International Conference in Lisbon.

October 1983 — Attempted to kill the Jordanian Ambassador to Italy in Rome.

October 1983 — Severely wounded the Jordanian Ambassador to India in New Delhi.

November 1983 — Attacked security guards in front of the Jordanian Embassy in Athens, killing one guard and wounding another.

December 1983 — Believed responsible for bombing the French Cultural Center in Izmir, Turkey.

February 1984 — Implicated in the Paris murder of the UAE Ambassador to France.

March 1984 — Assassinated a British diplomat in Athens.

November 1984 — Assassinated British High Commissioner in Bombay, India.

December 1984 — Killed Arafat-supporter Ismail Darwish in Rome.

December 1984 — Assassinated Jordanian diplomat in Bucharest.

March 1985 — Kidnaped British journalist Alec Collett in Beirut; Collett was reported to have been killed 1 year later, but information is not conclusive.

March 1985 — Attacked Rome offices of Alia, the Royal Jordanian Airlines, wounding three people. Also believed to be responsible for the simultaneous attacks on Alia offices in Athens and Nicosia.

April 1985 — Fired a rocket at an Alia airliner as it took off from Athens airport. Although the rocket did not explode, it left a hole in the fuselage.

July 1985 — Bombed and destroyed the office of British Airways in Madrid, killing a woman and wounding 27 other people. Five minutes later, attacked the Madrid offices of Alia, two blocks away, wounding two.

September 1985 — Conducted grenade attack against the Cafe de Paris in Rome, Italy, wounding 38.

September 1985 — Hijacked an Egyptian airliner to Malta, where 60 people were killed in the rescue attempt by Egyptian commandos.

December 1985 — Attacked the Rome and Vienna airports with machineguns and grenades. Sixteen people, including a child, were killed and 60 were injured.

Police inspect the scene of a December 1985 assault at the International Terminal of Rome's Leonardo da Vinci International Airport.

Dead victims lie on the floor of Leonardo da Vinci International Airport after the December 1985 assault by Abu Nidal terrorists.

September 1986 — Hijacked Pan Am flight 73 in Karachi, Pakistan: 17 were killed and over 150 wounded.

September 1986 — Attacked synagogue in Istanbul, killing 22 worshipers.

July 1987 — Claimed credit for bombing of restaurant in Qalqilya, West Bank, wounding 15 people.

November 1987 — Claimed to have seized a yacht off the coast of Israel and to have taken eight hostages.

March 1988 — A lone gunman attacked Alitalia airlines crew aboard a commuter bus in Bombay, India, seriously wounding the captain.

May 1988 — Detonated a car bomb in Nicosia, Cyprus, near the Israeli Embassy, killing 3 and injuring 17. ANO claimed it targeted the embassy in retaliation for the assassination of Abu Jihad.

May 1988 — In Khartoum, Sudan, gunmen killed 8 and wounded 21 in simultaneous attacks on the Acropole Hotel and the Sudan Club. Five British citizens killed and five Americans wounded.

Arab Organization of 15 May

Date Formed 1979.

Membership Very small.

Headquarters Not presently known.

Area of Operations Western Europe.

Leadership Husayn al-Umari (Abu Ibrahim).

Other Names 15 May.

Sponsors Not presently known.

Political Objectives/Target Audiences
- Destroy Israel.
- Intimidate moderate Palestinians and other Arabs who favor a negotiated settlement of the Palestinian issue.

Background

The 15 May takes its name from the founding date of Israel. Very little about the group is known outside of its vehement opposition to Israel. It uses distinctive and highly sophisticated explosives.

The 15 May group is apparently one of the small organizations that split from the Popular Front for the Liberation of Palestine (PFLP) in the late 1970s. Such splinter groups typically have vague organizational structures.

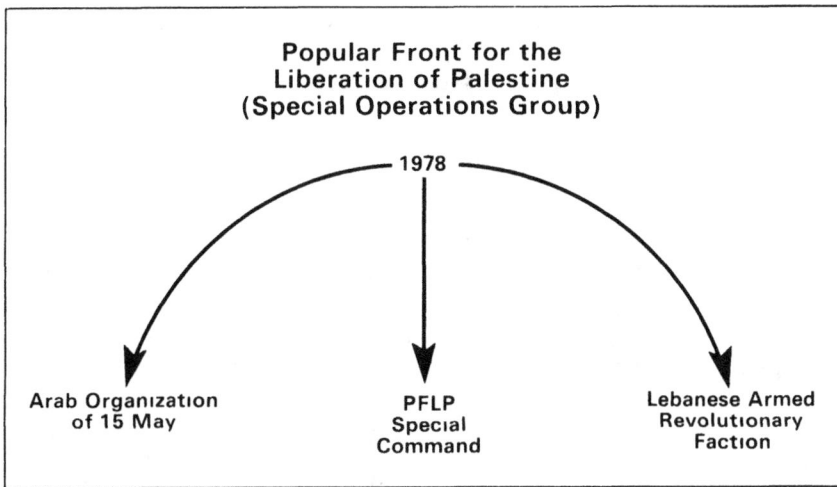

```
        Popular Front for the
        Liberation of Palestine
       (Special Operations Group)

              — 1978 —



Arab Organization          PFLP           Lebanese Armed
  of 15 May               Special         Revolutionary
                          Command            Faction
```

In 1978, the Popular Front for the Liberation of Palestine — Special Operations Group split into three groups, one of them the Arab Organization of 15 May.

The 15 May operations frequently target undefended public places. Airlines and airports are favored because of their international visibility.

No operations have been attributed definitively to the 15 May since 1983. Several recent bombings, however, raise the possibility that its members are active or have been absorbed into other terrorist organizations.

Selected Incident Chronology

January 1980 — Killed a 22-year-old Arab student and wounded a German national by bombing the Mount Royal Hotel in London.

May 1981 — Exploded a bomb outside the Rome office of El Al airlines.

August 1981 — Detonated a bomb near the El Al office at Leonardo da Vinci Airport outside Rome.

August 1981 — Exploded a bomb near the Israeli Embassy in Athens.

January 1982 — Killed 1 child and injured 46 people by bombing a Jewish restaurant in West Berlin.

August 1982 — Killed 1 and injured 14 with a time-delay bomb that exploded on an airplane just before it landed in Hawaii.

December 1983 — Attempted to blow up three airliners in flight. Bombs were discovered aboard two Israel-bound flights and a suitcase bomb was detected prior to being loaded onboard a flight from Rome to New York.

January 1984 — Attempted to blow up an El Al flight from Tel Aviv to Athens with a suitcase bomb. The attempt failed because of a technical failure in the bomb.

Democratic Front for the Liberation of Palestine (DFLP)

Date Formed 1969.

Estimated Membership 500.

Headquarters Previously Syria, presently unknown.

Area of Operations Lebanon and Israel.

Leadership Naif Hawatmeh, who depends heavily on Yasser Abed Rabbu, Qais Samarral (Abu Leila), and Abd-al-Karim Hammad (Abu Adnan).

Other Names Popular Democratic Front for the Liberation of Palestine (PDFLP).

Naif Hawatmeh, leader of the DFLP.

Yasser Abed Rabbu, number two man in the DFLP.

Sponsor Syria has provided some support, but the DFLP is intensely independent.

Political Objectives/Target Audiences
- Seek revolutionary change in the Arab world, especially in the conservative monarchies, as a precursor to the achievement of Palestinian objectives.
- Advocate an international stance that places the Palestinian struggle within a general world context of liberation in Africa, Asia, and Latin America.
- Repeatedly affirm its "hostility and resistance" to US policy in the region, its support for the nonaligned bloc, and its solidarity with all national liberation movements that fight against "imperialism" and racism.

Background

The DFLP is Marxist-Leninist and pro-Soviet and believes that the Palestinian national goal cannot be achieved without a revolution of the working class; elite members of the movement should not be separated from the masses, and the lower classes first should be educated in true socialism to carry on the battle.

At the spring 1977 Palestine National Council meeting, the DFLP gave full support to the Palestine national program, seeking creation of a Palestinian state from any territory liberated from Israel.

In mid-1979, the DFLP reportedly experienced an upsurge in its membership and an accompanying increase in influence. Although it remained a member of the Executive Committee of the Palestine Liberation Organization (PLO), the DFLP cooperated increasingly with anti-Arafat Palestinian extremists.

The DFLP strongly disapproved of the PLO leadership's failure to take more severe action against Anwar Sadat after his peace initiative.

Furthermore, the DFLP signed the Tripoli declaration in 1983, rejecting the Reagan and Fez peace plans and contact with the Israelis. The DFLP also did not support the Fatah rebels in 1983 or 1984, believing that their movement was damaging to the Palestine cause. In addition, the DFLP opposed the agreement between Yasir Arafat and King Hussein that called for a joint PLO-Jordanian position for peace negotiations with Israel.

The DFLP refused to join the Syrian-created Palestine National Salvation Front, but the Popular Front for the Liberation of Palestine (PFLP) did, leading to the breakup of the "Democratic Alliance" between the DFLP and PFLP.

DFLP operations always have taken place either inside Israel or the occupied territories. Typical acts are minor bombings and grenade attacks, as well as spectacular operations to seize hostages and attempt to negotiate the return of Israeli-held Palestinian prisoners.

Prior to the rift following the March 1987 Palestine National Council meeting in Algiers, Syria had provided most of the DFLP's outside support. The DFLP receives training in the Soviet Union and aid from Cuba. The DFLP is also in contact with members of the Nicaraguan Sandinista Liberation Front.

Selected Incident Chronology

May 1974 — Took over schoolhouse and massacred Israelis in Ma'alot after infiltrating using uniforms that resemble those of the Israel Defense Forces (IDF). Murdered 27 Israelis and wounded a total of 134.

November 1974 — Attacked the town of Bet She'an in Israel. Three terrorists barricaded themselves in a building with handgrenades and Kalashnikov rifles and demanded the release of 15 Palestinians.

July 1977 — Implicated in several bombings in Jerusalem and Tel Aviv.

January 1979 — Attempted to seize 230 civilians at a guest house in Ma'alot. The three terrorists, armed with Kalashnikovs and handgrenades, were killed by a routine IDF patrol.

March 1979 — Claimed responsibility for planting bombs in Israeli buses to protest President Carter's visit to Israel.

March 1982 — Claimed responsibility for a grenade attack in the Gaza Strip that killed an Israeli soldier and wounded three others.

February 1984 — Claimed responsibility for a grenade explosion in Jerusalem that wounded 21 people.

September 1985 — Attacked an Israeli bus near Hebron on the West Bank.

March 1986 — Several guerrillas, wearing IDF uniforms, attempted to infiltrate from Lebanon into Israel but were intercepted by an Israeli patrol.

May 1988 — Threw molotov cocktail at Industry and Trade Minister Ariel Sharon's car. Security forces uncovered several terrorist squads of DFLP and charged them with terrorist activities.

Fatah

Date Formed 1957.

Estimated Membership 6,000 in Lebanon and 5,000 scattered throughout the world.

Headquarters Tunis, Tunisia, serves as the symbolic international headquarters. The Fatah operates both overt and covert offices throughout the Middle East and Europe.

Area of Operations International. The Fatah's operational efforts are focused primarily against Israeli targets in Israel, Lebanon, and the occupied territories.

Leadership Yasir Arafat (Abu Ammar), Salah Khalaf (Abu Iyad).

Other Names The Fatah used the name Black September Organization (BSO) from 1971 to 1974 and the cover name al-Asifa (The Storm) in 1965. In recent years, Force 17, the Hawari group, and security elements of the Fatah have been involved in terrorist operations. The name Fatah is a backwards acronym for *Harakat al-Tahrir al Filistini,* which means "Palestine Liberation Movement" in Arabic.

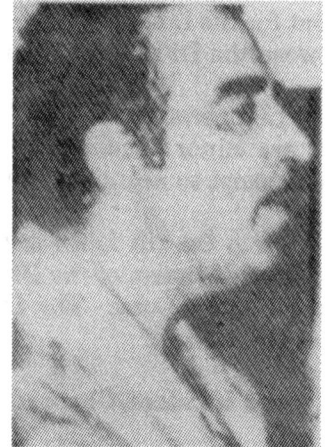

Fatah number two leader and security chief, Salah Khalaf.

Sponsors Palestine Liberation Organization, Palestinians abroad, most Arab states, China, the Soviet Union, and other Communist countries.

Political Objectives/Target Audiences
- Seek to establish an independent, secular Palestinian state; originally committed to recapturing all of Palestine, but now may accept a state based on a Gaza/West Bank formulation.
- Reject Camp David Accords.
- Recognize the Palestine Liberation Organization as the sole legitimate representative of the Palestinian people.

Background

Formed by Palestinian exiles in Kuwait in 1957, the Fatah surfaced in 1959 and began to mount raids into Israel in January 1965. After the 1967 Six-Day War, the Fatah, the military arm of the Palestine Liberation Organization (PLO), grew rapidly and eclipsed other Palestinian organizations. In 1969, Fatah leader Yasir Arafat assumed leadership of the PLO.

The increase in the Fatah's power after 1967 also created new problems for the organization, and in 1968 Israel initiated retaliatory strikes for Fatah operations against Israel by hitting Fatah locations in neighboring Jordan. The Fatah, meanwhile, began to compete directly with Jordanian authority in areas such as the Jordan River valley. These tensions culminated in September 1970 (referred to as "Black September" by radical Palestinians) when Jordanian authorities fought the Fatah to reassert control during a 9-day siege of Palestinian refugee camps in Jordan. Fatah-Jordanian friction continued through 1971, when the remainder of the Fatah forces were forced out of Jordan. Nearly all of Fatah's forces relocated to Lebanon.

Difficulties in conducting cross-border attacks against Israel from neighboring Jordan and Egypt prompted the Fatah to resort to international terrorism in 1971.

Fatah's strategy for using international terrorism changed in the wake of the 1973 Arab-Israeli War. Increased efforts on the part of the United States and other Western nations to forge a peace process in the Middle East caused Yasir Arafat to reconsider his political stance in the region. In an effort to improve Fatah's image with the United States and the West, Arafat decided to limit the employment of terrorist operations to Israel, Lebanon, and the occupied territories. The Fatah has not always adhered to this pledge, as Fatah elements have conducted terrorist operations against Israeli targets outside Israel and the occupied territories.

Israel's invasion of Lebanon in 1982 dealt a severe blow to Arafat's Fatah organization. After suffering a total military defeat in Lebanon, Fatah forces were allowed to leave Beirut en masse. The Fatah established its current headquarters in Tunisia in 1982. The effects of the 1 October 1985 Israeli air raid on PLO Headquarters in Tunis prompted a significant reduction in the Fatah presence in Tunisia. Today only a nominal PLO headquarters staff remains in Tunis. The primary concentrations of Fatah personnel are in Algeria, Lebanon, Iraq, Sudan, and the Yemen Arab Republic. Almost all intelligence and security personnel stationed in PLO diplomatic posts throughout the world are from the Fatah.

Selected Incident Chronology

March 1971 — A five-man Fatah team destroyed fuel tanks at Rotterdam oil docks, causing $1 million damage.

July 1971 — Attacked an Alia (Royal Jordanian Airlines) office in Rome.

July 1971 — Attacked an Alia plane at Cairo airport.

August 1971 — Hijacked an Alia plane to Algeria.

September 1971 — Attempted hijacking of an Alia plane from Beirut to Cairo.

November 1971 — Assassinated Jordanian Prime Minister Wasfi el-Tal in Cairo.

December 1971 — Attempted assassination of the Jordanian Ambassador to the United Kingdom in London.

February 1972 — Assassinated five Palestinian Arabs and one Jordanian in West Germany.

March 1972 — Attempted attack against King Hussein's London residence.

September 1972 — Eight terrorists seized dormitory of Israeli athletes at the Olympic Village in Munich. Eleven Israeli athletes murdered, 5 terrorists killed, 3 arrested but released following Lufthansa hijacking, October 1972.

September 1972 — Sent letter bombs from Amsterdam to Israel and Israeli missions in Paris, Geneva, Montreal, Vienna, Ottawa, Brussels, Kinshasa, Buenos Aires, Phnom Penh, and Washington, D.C.

November 1972 — Assassinated a Syrian journalist in France.

December 1972 — Captured the Israeli Embassy in Bangkok. Terrorists held six employees hostage, but released them after 19 hours.

January 1973 — Attacked the Jewish Agency building in Paris.

January 1973 — Murdered an Israeli citizen in Madrid.

March 1973 — Occupied Saudi Arabian Embassy in Sudan. Three Western diplomats, including the American and Belgian Ambassadors, killed. Terrorists captured.

March 1973 — Assassinated a Jewish businessman in Cyprus.

September 1973 — Attempted missile attack against El Al aircraft at Rome airport.

June 1974 — Three Fatah members landed by a small boat just south of the Israeli town of Nahariya and killed four Israelis and wounded eight others before being killed by Israeli troups.

September 1975 — Occupied Egyptian Embassy in Madrid. Terrorists seized six diplomats whom they threatened to kill unless Egypt withdrew from Geneva talks and condemned interim agreement with Israel. Terrorists took hostages to Algiers, where they were released.

March 1978 — Sabotaged the Iraqi Embassy in Belgium.

July 1978 — Attempted assassination of Iraqi Ambassador to the United Kingdom.

August 1978 — Attempted assassination of Iraqi Consul in Karachi, Pakistan.

April 1985 — The coastal freighter *Atavarius* was intercepted and sunk while trying to infiltrate a Fatah raiding force into Israel. Twenty Palestinians killed and 8 captured.

September 1985 — Seized and murdered three Israeli hostages in Larnaca, Cyprus.

October 1985 — Kidnaped and murdered two Israeli sailors in Madrid.

February 1986 — Force 17 claimed responsibility for a bus bombing in Israel that wounded six people.

June 1986 — A Palestinian was killed while attempting to place a bomb in Jerusalem; Force 17 claimed responsibility.

July 1986 — Fatah operatives in Morocco arrested while planning terrorist attack.

September 1986 — An Israeli citizen was stabbed to death in a market in Gaza. The murder was claimed by Force 17.

February 1987 — Nine people were injured by a bomb placed on a bus en route to Jerusalem from Haifa. Force 17 claimed the attack.

July 1987 — Force 17 claimed a bus bombing in Israel that injured two people.

July 1987 — Anti-Arafat Palestinian cartoonist assassinated in London. Force 17 has been implicated in the attack.

August 1987 — One Israeli was killed and two were wounded in two separate shooting incidents in Gaza. Both attacks were claimed by Force 17.

Hizballah (Islamic Jihad)

Date Formed 1983.

Estimated Membership Approximately 3,000 full-time members, with perhaps as many as 500 directly involved in terrorist activity.

Headquarters West Beirut and Bekaa Valley, Lebanon.

Area of Operations Middle East and Europe.

Leadership A Consultative Council (Shura) that reports to Iran. Leading officials are Husayn Musawi, Abbas Musawi, Subhi Tufayli, Muhammed Rad, Naim Qasim, Muhammed Fennish, and Iranian Revolutionary Guard personnel stationed in Lebanon. Shaykh Muhammad Husayn Fadlallah is the overall spiritual leader of the movement.

Other Names Islamic Jihad, Party of God, Revolutionary Justice Organization, Organization of the Oppressed.

Muhammad Husayn Fadlallah, spiritual leader of the Hizballah.

Sponsor Iran.

Political Objectives/Target Audiences
- Establish a revolutionary Shi'a Islamic state in Lebanon, modeled after Iran.
- Eliminate non-Islamic influences and force Western interests out of the region.
- Become institutionalized as Lebanon's principal Islamic movement.

Background

The Hizballah is a political, social, and military organization that gives focus and general identity in Lebanon to Ayatollah Khomeini's Islamic militancy. The Hizballah espouses an intense hatred of any influence that does not support its views of Shi'a Muslim ideology. An element within the Hizballah actively employs terrorism as a tactic to support the group's political and religious goals.

The Hizballah movement was born as a result of the merger of Husayn Musawi's Islamic Amal and the Lebanese branch of the Da'wa Party in 1982-83. Three area councils — for Beirut, the Bekaa Valley, and south Lebanon — oversee activities in their respective geographic areas. Series of functional area committees play roles in policy recommendation and execution. The Shura functions as the principal governing body on day-to-day matters but actually exists to advise Iran on the unique situation of the Islamic movement in Lebanon. Hizballah elements receive training in the Bekaa Valley of eastern Lebanon. Through this connection, Iranian Revolutionary Guardsmen provide political indoctrination, financing, and material support. The Hizballah and the Revolutionary Guards work in close concert on terrorist operations.

The Hizballah itself seldom directly claims specific terrorist acts, but does so under codenames such as Islamic Jihad.

Iran created the Hizballah movement, and some of the Hizballah's cadres are directly tied to the Iranian Revolutionary Guard contingent in Lebanon. The Hizballah's official spokesman, Ibrahim al-Amin, reportedly has stated that he has no influence over certain cadres, who receive orders directly from the Iranian Revolutionary Guard.

Selected Incident Chronology

April 1983 — Committed suicide car bomb attack on the US Embassy in Beirut; operation claimed under the name of the Islamic Jihad. Forty-nine killed and 120 wounded.

The US Marine Headquarters in Beirut, Lebanon, was destroyed by a truck bomb attack in late October 1983.

British soldiers aid in rescue operations at the site of the demolished US Marine Headquarters after the October 1983 truck bombing that killed 241 Marines.

October 1983 — "Kamikazi" terrorists drove two trucks carrying explosives into the US Marine and French military barracks in Beirut, killing 241 US and 56 French. Islamic Jihad claimed responsibility.

November 1983 — A Hizballah operative drove a car bomb into the Israeli headquarters in Tyre, South Lebanon, causing numerous casualties.

December 1983 — Staged a series of car bomb attacks against the US and French Embassies in Kuwait.

January 1984 — Murdured American University of Beirut President Malcom Kerr, a US citizen. Islamic Jihad claimed responsibility.

January 1984 — Kidnaped Husayn Farrash, Saudi diplomat; released May 1985.

February 1984 — Assassinated former Iranian General Gholam Oveisi (Martial Law Administrator for Tehran under the Shah) and his brother in Paris.

February 1984 — Kidnaped Frank Regier, US professor; he was subsequently rescued in April 1984.

March 1984 — Kidnaped Jeremy Levin, US journalist; he escaped in February 1985.

March 1984 — Kidnaped William Buckley, US diplomat; he was reported killed in October 1985. Islamic Jihad claimed responsibility.

May 1984 — Kidnaped Reverend Benjamin Weir, US citizen; he was released in September 1985.

September 1984 — Committed suicide truck bombing of the US Embassy Annex in East Beirut. Twenty-three persons, including 2 Americans, were killed. Islamic Jihad claimed responsibility.

December 1984 — Hijacked Kuwait Air flight 221 to Tehran. Murdered two US Agency for International Development officials.

January 1985 — Kidnaped Father Lawrence Martin Jenco, US citizen; he was released in July 1986. Islamic Jihad claimed responsibility.

March 1985 — Kidnaped Geoffrey Nash, UK professor; he was released shortly thereafter.

March 1985 — Kidnaped Brian Levick, UK businessman; he was released shortly thereafter.

March 1985 — Kidnaped AP journalist Terry Anderson, US citizen.

March 1985 — Kidnaped Marcel Fontaine, Danielle Perez, and Marcel Carton, French diplomats; Perez was released shortly thereafter.

May 1985 — Kidnaped French citizens Jean-Paul Kaufmann, journalist, and Michel Seurat, researcher; Seurat was killed in March 1986.

May 1985 — Kidnaped David Jacobsen, US citizen, American University of Beirut director. Islamic Jihad claimed responsibility. He was released November 1986.

May 1985 — Murder of British citizen Dennis Hill (Hizballah suspected).

June 1985 — Kidnaped Thomas Sutherland, US citizen, American University of Beirut dean. Islamic Jihad claimed responsibility.

June 1985 — Hijacked TWA flight 847 en route to Athens. US Navy diver Robert Stethem murdered. Hizballah held 39 US citizens hostage for 17 days in Beirut.

July 1985 — Simultaneously bombed Northwest Orient Airlines office and a synagogue in Copenhagen. One person killed and 26 injured. Islamic Jihad claimed responsibility.

December 1985 — Rocked Paris with a series of bombings. Hizballah members arrested.

March 1986 — Kidnaped four French television news team members: Philippe Rochot, Georges Hansen, Aurel Cornea, and Jean-Louis Normandin. Rochot and Hansen were released in June 1986, Cornea in December 1986, and Normandin in November 1987.

April 1986 — Bombed Northwest Orient Airlines office in Stockholm. Hizballah suspected.

April 1986 — Kidnaped two Cypriot students.

September 1986 — Kidnaped Frank Reed, US citizen.

A TWA Boeing 727 sits on the tarmac at Beirut International Airport after it was hijacked by Islamic Jihad terrorists in June 1985. One American, Navy diver Robert Stethem, was murdered by the terrorists.

September 1986 — Kidnaped Joseph Cicippio, US citizen.

September 1986 — Assassinated Col Christian Goutierre, French military attache, in East Beirut (Hizballah suspected).

September 1986 — Committed another series of bombings in Paris. French police arrested a number of Hizballah members.

October 1986 — Kidnaped Edward Austin Tracy. The "Revolutionary Justice Organization" claimed responsibility.

January 1987 — In two separate incidents, kidnaped two German businessman, Rudolph Cordes and Alfred Schmidt; Schmidt was released in September 1987, and Cordes in September 1988.

January 1987 — Kidnaped Anglican Church envoy Terry Waite.

January 1987 — Kidnaped Beirut University College professors Jesse Turner, Alan Steen, Robert Polhill — US citizens — and Mithileshwar Singh. Singh was released in October 1988.

June 1987 — Kidnaped Charles Glass, US journalist; he escaped in August 1987.

July 1987 — Hijacked Air Afrique jetliner on flight from Brazzaville to Paris. One French citizen was murdered.

February 1988 — Kidnaped United Nations Military Observer Lt Col Richard Higgins, USMC.

April 1988 — Hijacked Kuwaiti Airlines flight 422 from Bangkok to Kuwait and diverted it to Iran. Plane refueled, flew to Cyprus, and subsequently flew to Algeria. The hijackers secretly escaped.

Lebanese Armed Revolutionary Faction (LARF)

Date Formed 1979.

Estimated Membership 25.

Headquarters Northern Lebanon.

Area of Operations Western Europe, Lebanon.

Leadership George Ibrahim Abdallah (AKA Salah al-Masri or Abdul-Qader Saadi).

Other Names FARL (in French).

Political Objectives/Target Audiences
- Establish a Marxist-Leninist state in Lebanon.
- Force the United States, Israel, and France to withdraw their presence from Lebanon.
- Demonstrate "anti-Zionist" solidarity with the Palestinian movement by attacking Israeli interests, primarily in France.

Background

The Marxist-Leninist LARF is a pro-Palestinian, anti-Zionist organization with roots in the Popular Front for the Liberation of Palestine (PFLP). However, few if any of LARF's members are of Palestinian origin. Rather, the group consists mostly of Lebanese Christians from the villages of Qubayyat and Andaqat in northern Lebanon.

The LARF — along with the Popular Front for the Liberation of Palestine — Special Command (PFLP-SC) and the 15 May Organization — arose from the remnants of the PFLP Special Operations Group after its leader, Wadi Haddad, died in 1978. George Ibrahim Abdallah is believed to have founded the LARF in 1978-79, and its first operations may have been against Christian Phalange targets in Lebanon in 1979-80. Abdallah moved LARF operations to Europe sometime around mid-1980.

A captured cache of arms of the Lebanese Armed Revolutionary Faction (LARF). The cache includes communications and electronic equipment, Czechoslovak VP-71 machine pistols, and Semtex plastic explosives.

The LARF established its reputation with a series of killings of US and Israeli diplomats in France. The group has conducted its most lethal operations in Western Europe. The LARF has established an extensive network of safehouses, bank accounts, and arms caches throughout Europe.

In 1984, a series of significant arrests by Italian and French police, including the capture of LARF leader George Ibrahim Abdallah, who was sentenced to life imprisonment in 1987, caused serious damage to the group. As a result, the LARF reportedly has retreated to Lebanon and reestablished its base of operations there, at least temporarily.

Within Lebanese politics, the LARF opposes the existing government and may still have a strong relationship with the PFLP. The LARF also may enjoy a cooperative relationship with the Hizballah. In Europe, there were links between the LARF and the French terrorist group Direct Action.

LARF tactics vary widely. In Lebanon tactics have included letter, package, and car bombs and kidnapings. In Western Europe, the LARF has conducted assassination attempts and car bombings.

It is reasonable to expect that the LARF may continue attacks on those countries holding LARF prisoners (France and Italy), or against any country assisting in the legal proceedings against jailed LARF members, such as the United States and Israel.

Selected Incident Chronology

November 1981 — Attempted to assassinate US Charge d'Affairs Christian Chapman in Paris.

January 1982 — Murdered Assistant US Army Attache, LTC Charles Ray, while he stood on a Paris sidewalk.

April 1982 — Conducted machinegun attack on Israeli Embassy in Paris and murdered an Israeli diplomat.

August 1982 — Left a bomb outside the Paris home of US Commercial Counselor in Paris. One bomb disposal technician was killed and another injured in trying to disarm the device.

September 1982 — Wounded Israeli Defense Purchasing Mission officer Amos Manel and two other individuals in bomb attack on their vehicle in Paris.

December 1983 — Israeli Charge d'Affairs Millo was assassinated in Malta. Although the incident remains unattributed, it was similar in style to other LARF attacks.

February 1984 — May have assisted in the murder of Leamon Hunt, Director General of the Multinational Force and Observers, in Rome (the Italian Red Brigades is also strongly suspected).

March 1985 — Kidnaped the head of the French Cultural Center, Gilles Peyrolles, in Tripoli, Lebanon. He was released a week later.

June 1986 — Claimed credit for bombing Italian military attache's car in East Beirut.

September-December 1986 — Played a role in a series of bombing campaigns that rocked Paris, leaving 15 killed and over 150 wounded.

Organization of the Armed Arab Struggle (OAAS)

Date Formed About 1978.

Estimated Membership Very small.

Headquarters Libya or Syria.

Area of Operations Western Europe, Middle East.

Leadership Carlos (Illych Ramirez Sanchez).

Other Names Carlos Apparat.

Sponsors Popular Front for the Liberation of Palestine (PFLP) and Libya.

Political Objectives/Target Audiences

- Conduct terrorism in support of general Arab revolutionary movements.
- Conduct terrorism against West European nations in retaliation for "anti-Arab" Middle East policies practiced by these nations.
- Maintain the myth of Carlos as a terrorist par excellence.

Background

Carlos was born in Venezuela, the son of a prominent Marxist lawyer. He became involved in revolutionary activities at an early age and studied at Patrice Lumumba University in the Soviet Union (from which he was expelled for not being serious in his studies).

Carlos was recruited by the PFLP in Lebanon in the early 1970s and served in its European unit. Carlos was involved extensively with the PFLP — Special Operations Group (PFLP-SOG) of Wadi Haddad in Lebanon in the late 1970s. He was, therefore, one of the original trainers of the three organizations that sprang up after Haddad's death in 1978 — the PFLP-SC (Special Command), the Lebanese Armed Revolutionary Faction (LARF), and the 15 May Organization.

Carlos became established as a leader in the PFLP and engineered the 1975 OPEC oil ministers hostage incident in Vienna. This operation included support and participation by European terrorist organizations such as the West German Baader Meinhof Gang. After this incident, he apparently went into semiretirement and became an adviser to various Middle East terrorist groups.

Although unconfirmed, Carlos was reported to be in Damascus in 1984 training Syrian intelligence agents. Firm identification of Carlos is difficult because he is believed to have undergone extensive plastic surgery. He has been reported in many locations in the Middle East over the last several years, most frequently in Tripoli, Libya, and Damascus, Syria. There also are unconfirmed reports that Carlos may be dead.

The OAAS came to prominence in 1983 in a series of attacks directed against French interests, probably in retaliation for French military involvement in Beirut. Therefore, it may be that the OAAS was the cover name employed by Carlos for this specific series of attacks. Nonetheless, the attacks demonstrated Carlos' ability to attack targets in the Middle East and Europe, indicating an existing network in both regions. Although operations under the OAAS name apparently ceased as of January 1984, it is possible that the Carlos Apparat still exists. If so, the Carlos Apparat may be providing unspecified assistance to the European and Middle Eastern terrorist groups with which it enjoyed good relations in the past. Sponsorship of the Carlos Apparat/OAAS has come from Libya and the PFLP.

Selected Incident Chronology

August 1983 — Killed 1 and wounded 23 in a bombing of the French Cultural Center in West Berlin.

December 1983 — Killed 2 and wounded 45 with a suitcase bomb at a Marseilles railroad station.

December 1983 — Exploded a bomb aboard the French "bullet train" that killed three and injured four. (This incident also was claimed by the French terrorist group Direct Action, which may have been cooperating with the OAAS.)

January 1984 — Killed one with a bomb blast at the French Cultural Center in Tripoli, Lebanon.

Palestine Liberation Front (PLF)

Date Formed 1977 (split in 1983 and further split in 1984).

Estimated Membership 300 (among 3 factions).

Headquarters One faction (Tal'at Yaqub) in Syria, another (Abu al Abbas) in Iraq, and the third (Abd al Fatah Ghanem) in Libya.

Area of Operations Lebanon, Israel, and Europe.

Leadership Muhammed Abu al Abbas, Abd al Fatah Ghanem, and Tal'at Yaqub; each heads one of the three major factions.

Other Names Front for the Liberation of Palestine (FLP).

Sponsors Syria, Libya, and Iraq.

Political Objectives/Target Audiences
- The PLF factions led by Tal'at Yaqub and Abd al Fatah Ghanem oppose Yasir Arafat's leadership of the Palestine Liberation Organization (PLO) and are rejectionist. The third faction, led by Muhammed Abu al Abbas, supports Arafat's leadership, but has opposed some of Arafat's peace moves.
- In general, the three factions of the PLF share the basic goals of dismantling the current state of Israel, terrorizing Israel by direct attacks on its soil, and establishing an independent Palestinian state in place of Israel.

Background

Although originally part of the Popular Front for the Liberation of Palestine — General Command (PFLP-GC), the PLF was established under Muhammed Abu al Abbas, in opposition to PFLP-GC leader Ahmad Jibril's support for the Syrian incursion into Lebanon in June 1976. After unsuccessfully attempting to obtain control of the PFLP-GC in September 1976, the PLF was split from the PFLP-GC officially by PLO Chairman Yasir Arafat in April 1977. The PLF was established with Iraqi support, and its existence as an independent group was recognized when it obtained seats on the Palestine National Council in 1981 with its headquarters in Damascus.

Near the end of 1983, the PLF itself split into factions when Abu al Abbas felt that his organization had become too close to Syria. Leaving Damascus, along with many supporters Abu al Abbas went to Tunis to align himself with Arafat and the mainstream Fatah organization. Following the *Achille Lauro* incident, the Abu al Abbas faction relocated to Baghdad at the request of the Tunisian Government.

The parts of the PLF remaining in Damascus were further split in January 1984 when Abd al Fatah Ghanem attempted a takeover of the PLF offices and held Tal'at Yaqub, Secretary General of the PLF, hostage. Through Syrian intervention, Yaqub was released, and Ghanem formed his own faction with ties to Libya. Yaqub's faction joined the Palestine National Salvation Front and is generally aligned with Syria.

Operationally, the PLF has demonstrated creativity and technical acumen. The group has employed balloons and hang gliders for airborne operations and a civilian passenger ship for an attempted seaborne infiltration operation. Similar operations against Israel are expected to continue.

The *Achille Lauro* hijacking in October 1985 — followed by the airborne intercept of the PLF operatives by US Navy jets over the Mediterranean Sea and the subsequent conviction of the terrorists — created international condemnation of Abu al Abbas and his faction of the PLF.

Selected Incident Chronology

July 1978 — Kidnaped 51 UNIFIL soldiers in Tyre; forced by the Fatah to release them several hours later.

September 1978 — Three PLF terrorists were captured in northern Israel; they had intended a hostage-taking operation with the goal of seeking the release of PLF members imprisoned in Israel.

April 1979 — Four PLF terrorists landed from the sea near Nahariyah, intending to seize Israeli hostages to be used in exchange for guerrilla prisoners. The terrorists killed a man and his daughter in their apartment, as well as an Israeli policeman. Two terrorists were killed during the fighting and two were captured.

August 1979 — Attempted unsuccessfully to infiltrate by sea near Rosh Haniqra, Israel. Three terrorists were captured and one killed.

July 1980 — Attempted unsuccessfully to infiltrate into Israel using a hot-air balloon. The balloon exploded after takeoff, killing one terrorist.

March 1981 — Attempted to send two one-man hang gliders into Israel. Both were captured.

April 1981 — Attempted unsuccessfully to infiltrate Israel using a hot-air balloon. The balloon was shot down, and two PLF operatives were killed. Documents found on the terrorists indicated that their mission was to take hostages in exchange for imprisoned PLF members in Israel.

June 1984 — A squad from the Ghanem faction was captured in northern Israel, believed to be on another hostage-taking operation.

October 1985 — Hijacked Italian cruise ship *Achille Lauro*. After holding hostages for 2 days and killing one wheelchair-bound US passenger, the terrorists and leader Abu al Abbas surrendered in exchange for an Egyptian promise of safe passage. They were apprehended at a NATO airbase in Italy after US aircraft intercepted and forced down the Egyptian airliner that was flying them to safehaven. Abu al Abbas was soon released by the Italians. The four PLF terrorists responsible for the *Achille Lauro* incident were tried and convicted, and are now serving prison sentences in Italy.

Leon Klinghoffer's body is prepared for return to the United States after he was murdered by PLF terrorists during the Achille Lauro hijacking.

Popular Front for the Liberation of Palestine (PFLP)

Date Formed 11 December 1967.

Estimated Membership Approximately 1,000.

Headquarters Previously Syria.

Area of Operations Europe, Middle East.

Leadership Dr. George Habash.

Other Names None Known.

Sponsors South Yemen, Libya.

Political Objectives/Target Audiences

PFLP leader Dr. George Habash.

- Create an image of the Palestinian struggle as part of the world-wide Marxist-Leninist revolution.
- Liberate Palestine with "armed struggle."
- Establish a Marxist-Leninist government in Palestine.
- Oppose all efforts at a negotiated settlement of the Israeli-Palestinian issue.

Background

The PFLP was formed after the Arab defeat in the 1967 Arab-Israeli War. George Habash created the PFLP as a merger of three formerly independent groups — the Arab Nationalist Movement's Heroes of Return, the National Front for the Liberation of Palestine, and the independent Palestine Liberation Front (as distinguished from the currently existing Palestine Liberation Front). Referred to by his followers as *al-Hakim* ("the physician" or "the wise man"), Habash has remained consistent in his position towards solving the Palestinian problem — the total liberation of Palestine.

The PFLP established itself early as one of the most violent Palestinian terrorist groups. It concurrently sought to establish strong ties to other Marxist revolutionary organizations. Those links facilitated PFLP European operations that gave the group much of its notoriety. Habash strongly favors well-publicized attacks on civilian targets, and the PFLP reputation for ruthlessness was built on that strategy.

As a result of ideological inflexibility, internal disputes, and personality conflicts, the PFLP spawned several splinter groups, including the PFLP — General Command and the Democratic Front for the Liberation of Palestine (DFLP).

The PFLP was one of the most active international terrorist organizations in the early 1970s. As a result of publicity that attracted condemnation even from Communist Bloc countries, the PFLP ceased international operations and focused on developing conventional and guerrilla forces for use against Israeli targets.

Selected Incident Chronology

July 1968 — Hijacked an El Al airliner en route from Rome to Israel.

September 1969 — Conducted simultaneous hijackings of three airliners. Two were flown to Jordan and one to Egypt, and all three were blown up in front of television cameras.

May 1972 — Used Japanese Red Army terrorists to conduct a machinegun attack in the Lod Airport terminal building in Tel Aviv. Twenty-seven civilians, including 16 Puerto Rican tourists visiting the Holy Land, were killed.

July 1973 — Hijacked a Japanese airliner to Libya and blew it up.

December 1974 — Threw handgrenades into crowded Tel Aviv theater, killing 3 and wounding 54.

June 1976 — Hijacked an Air France airliner to Entebbe, Uganda, where four civilians were killed during the rescue operation by Israeli paratroopers.

August 1976 — Killed four passengers on an El Al airliner in Istanbul.

October 1977 — Hijacked a Lufthansa airliner to Mogadishu, Somalia, demanding release of terrorists being held in West German jails. West German commandos moved on the plane, killing three terrorists and capturing a fourth. One commando and four passengers wounded.

April 1979 — After a foiled attempt to take over an El Al aircraft at Zaventem airport in Brussels, Belgium, threw a gasoline bomb and a handgrenade into a visitors' area, wounding five Belgians, and entered an airport restaurant, shooting and wounding seven customers.

March 1984 — Killed three passengers in an attack on a bus in Ashdod, Israel.

April 1984 — Killed one and wounded eight passengers in bus hijacking in Ashkelon, Israel.

May 1985 — Claimed responsibility for bombing an Israeli bus.

November 1986 — Stabbed to death a 22-year-old yeshiva student on a street in the old city of Jerusalem.

May 1987 — Claimed responsibility for rocket attack on the town of Metullah in northern Galilee.

Popular Front for the Liberation of Palestine — General Command (PFLP-GC)

Date Formed 1968.

Estimated Membership 500.

Headquarters Syria.

Area of Operations Middle East, especially Lebanon, Jordan, and Israel.

Leadership Ahmad Jibril.

Other Names None.

Sponsors Syria, Libya.

Political Objectives/Target Audiences
- Destroy Israel and establish an independent Palestine in its place.
- Terrorize Israeli citizens, especially those in border regions and occupied territories.
- Oppose any moves toward moderation in the Palestinian movement.

Background

Ahmad Jibril formed the PFLP-GC in 1968 when he became disenchanted with George Habash's leadership of the PFLP. An officer in the Syrian Army, Jibril was interested in developing conventional military capabilities to complement PFLP-GC terrorist activities. As a result, the PFLP-GC always has been known for its conventional military expertise. In addition to ground infiltration capabilities, the PFLP-GC is developing air and naval infiltration capabilities as well.

PFLP-GC terrorist activities include using letter bombs and conducting major cross-border operations directed at Israeli targets. The PFLP-GC also has shared its terrorist expertise with other international groups, such as the Armenian Secret Army for the Liberation of Armenia, as well as European groups who have sent members to Lebanon for training.

The PFLP-GC arsenal includes sophisticated weapons such as Soviet SA-7 antiaircraft missiles, heavy artillery, and light aircraft such as motorized hang gliders and ultralights. The Communist Bloc countries also provide small arms such as Kalashnikov assault rifles and RPG-7 antitank rockets, but Syria or Libya may serve as the conduit for such support.

The PFLP-GC actively participated in the Lebanese conflict, including sniping attacks that injured US Marines who were members of the peacekeeping forces in Beirut in 1982-83. In addition, the group attacked Israeli citizens and interests with operations launched from Lebanon. The PFLP-GC also occasionally recruits West Bank Palestinians to conduct terrorist attacks inside Israel.

In May 1985, the PFLP-GC engineered an exchange of 3 Israeli soldiers for 1,150 Palestinian prisoners held by Israel. The Israelis were captured by the PFLP-GC near Beirut in September 1982. This was one of the few operations conducted by the PFLP-GC since 1978, although the group may have broken out of its relative dormancy with the spectacular hang glider attack near Qiryat Shemona in November 1987.

Selected Incident Chronology

July 1968 — Hijacked an El Al airliner en route from Rome to Tel Aviv, diverting it to Algeria for a lengthy hostage incident. The terrorists demanded the release of 1,000 prisoners in Israel. Weeks later, Israel released 16 Arab infiltrators as a "humanitarian" gesture.

February 1969 — Machinegunned an El Al airliner as it was about to take off from Zurich for Tel Aviv.

August 1969 — Hijacked a TWA airliner en route to Athens and Tel Aviv and forced it to land in Damascus, where the passengers were evacuated and the plane was destroyed by a time bomb.

April 1974 — Attacked Qiryat Shemona, Israel, killing 18 and wounding 16 in an apartment building. The three terrorists also killed two members of the Israeli assault force that engaged in a 4-hour gun battle with the terrorists. All three terrorists were killed, probably by their own grenades. The intention of the operation was to secure the release of 100 captured Palestinians being held in Israeli prisons.

April 1978 — Kidnaped an Israeli soldier in southern Lebanon. In March 1979, Israel exchanged 66 Palestinian prisoners for the soldier and 10 others in the occupied territories.

September 1982 — Seized 3 Israeli soldiers in Beirut, held them until May 1985, and then exchanged them for 1,150 Palestinian prisoners held by Israel.

February 1986 — Ahmad Jibril held press conference in Libya, stating that "there will be no safety for any traveler on an Israeli or US airliner."

April 1986 — Claimed responsibility for a firebomb thrown at a bus in Jerusalem.

June 1987 — At central bus station in Tel Aviv, Israeli bomb squad defused a bomb suspected of being placed there by the PFLP-GC.

November 1987 — A member of the PFLP-GC successfully penetrated Israel from Lebanon, using a powered hang glider. The terrorist killed six Israeli soldiers and wounded seven others in the attack.

Popular Struggle Front (PSF)

Date Formed 1967.

Estimated Membership 200.

Headquarters Moves between Syria and Libya.

Area of Operations Lebanon and Israeli-occupied territories.

Leadership Dr. Samir Ghawshah.

Other Names Palestine Popular Struggle Front (PPSF).

Sponsors Libya and Syria.

Political Objectives/Target Audiences
- Call for an "armed struggle" to liberate Palestine, eliminate Israel, and create a democratic, secular state in all of the former British Mandate territory of Palestine.
- Oppose the creation of a ministate on the occupied West Bank and the Gaza Strip.
- Emphasize an Arab nationalist approach in combating "reactionary, Zionist imperialist" forces.

Background

A veteran Palestinian activist, Bahjat Abu Gharbiyah, founded the PSF in cooperation with Major Fayez Hamdan of the Palestine Liberation Army. Gharbiyah was involved with the first Palestine Liberation Organization (PLO) leadership after 1964, but suspended PSF activities and participation on the PLO Executive Committee after the Jordanian suppression of 1970. The PSF was revived after the October 1973 War.

In 1974, Gharbiyah resigned and was succeeded by Samir Ghawshah. At that point, the PSF joined the Rejection Front and retained the rejectionist stance of scorning a Palestinian state in the West Bank and Gaza, as well as advocating closer cooperation with various other guerrilla and leftist movements.

Since the 1982 Israeli invasion of Lebanon, the PSF has come under stronger Syrian influence. The PSF also joined the Palestine National Salvation Front in opposition to the Arafat-Hussein accord of February 1985.

The PSF currently is headquartered in Damascus and primarily based in Lebanon's Bekaa Valley. The Israel Air Force claimed in 1985 to have attacked PSF bases located near Bar Elias in the Bekaa Valley and in Shamlan, near Beirut.

The PSF has undertaken several rocket attacks and cross-border operations into Israel, and has claimed responsibility for many actions that were never confirmed. The group also kidnaped a US Army colonel in Beirut in 1975.

Selected Incident Chronology

May 1975 — Bombed Ein Fesh'ha, an Israeli resort.

June-July 1975 — Kidnaped a US Army colonel in Beirut and turned him over to the Popular Front for the Liberation of Palestine — General Command after food was delivered to Palestinian refugee camps in Beirut.

March 1979 — Claimed responsibility for an explosion on a tourist bus at the Intercontinental Hotel in Jerusalem, and attempted an operation, probably intended to be hostage taking, on the West Bank to protest President Carter's visit to Egypt and Israel.

June 1985 — Claimed responsibility for rocket attack on the northern Israel town of Metullah.

September 1985 — Claimed responsibility for an attack at a swimming pool in Athens. The PSF member who made the claim incorrectly stated that 75 American soldiers were killed or wounded in the attack; despite the claim, the Abu Nidal Organization is believed to be responsible for the incident, in which 18 deaf-mute British tourists were wounded.

April 1987 — Claimed responsibility for rocket attack on northern Israel.

Sa'iqa

Date Formed 1968.

Estimated Membership 2,000.

Headquarters Syria.

Area of Operations Middle East, Western Europe.

Leadership Issam al-Qadi, Sami al-Attari.

Other Names The Thunderbolt, Eagles of the Palestinian Revolution.

Sponsors Syria.

Political Objectives/Target Audiences
- Provide a mechanism for Syria to control and influence the Palestinian movement.
- Eliminate Israel and replace it with a pro-Syrian Palestinian state.
- Establish a pro-Syrian Palestinian Army.

Background

The ruling Baath Party in Syria established the Sa'iqa in 1968 to manipulate the Palestinian liberation movement to achieve Syrian political goals. Sa'iqa's role as a member of the Palestinian movement is not as important, though, as is its role as a Syrian surrogate and an integral part of the Syrian military.

Sa'iqa's standing within the Palestinian movement was always weak, especially after its support of the Syrian intervention in Lebanon in 1976. Sa'iqa activity temporarily increased after the 1979-80 Egyptian-Israeli accords, when Sa'iqa targeting was expanded to include both Israeli and Egyptian interests.

The Sa'iqa also has been employed by Syria to attack regime opponents, such as the Muslim Brotherhood, in locations outside Syria.

Selected Incident Chronology

September 1971 — Attacked a train carrying Soviet Jews in Austria.

September 1975 — Sa'iqa operative Abdallah Mustafa Ataya, who took part in unsuccessful terrorist operation in Amerfoot, Netherlands, sentenced to 1 year in prison for weapons charges and expelled to Damascus in June 1976.

March 1979 — Wounded 20 Jewish students in 2 bombings in Paris.

May 1979 — Killed 2 Israelis and wounded 32 others in an attack on the northern border town of Tiberias.

July 1979 — Occupied the Egyptian Embassy in Ankara, Turkey. Two guards were killed and 20 hostages were taken in the attack.

May 1984 — The press in Nicosia, Cyprus, reported that two Arabs belonging to the Syrian-backed Palestinian organization Sa'iqa murdered a supporter of Yasir Arafat.

August 1985 — Claimed responsibility for throwing a bomb at a civilian Israeli vehicle on the Nablus-Tulkarm road. The driver was seriously injured.

July 1987 — Claimed responsibility for attempted infiltration of Israel by sea. Two terrorists killed and one captured.

West European Terrorism

Although many spectacular terrorist acts have taken place in the Middle East, US citizens are more numerous in Western Europe and have been targeted more consistently there. Despite the number of indigenous terrorist groups in Western Europe, the most serious terrorist threat there actually comes from various Middle Eastern terrorist groups described in the previous section.

Most indigenous West European terrorists are "urban terrorists." The most notorious groups are reminiscent of 19th century anarchists — they espouse a revolutionary philosophy, usually some form of Marxism-Leninism; they are dedicated to overthrowing the existing government and social order, but are inarticulate about their vision of a substitute system; and they are mostly small.

Lethal terrorist acts usually are carried out by a small nucleus. Some groups like the West German Red Army Faction, the Italian Red Brigades, and the Greek 17 November are highly structured. Others like the West German Revolutionary Cells are loosely organized. All attack the state, its representatives, and symbols of the established order, and all target the United States and NATO as representatives of "imperialism." They characterize the US military presence in Europe as an occupying force, justifying attacks on US military personnel and facilities.

Their targets usually are selected very deliberately rather than indiscriminately, and involve consideration of the symbolic value of the target. Members of these indigenous groups

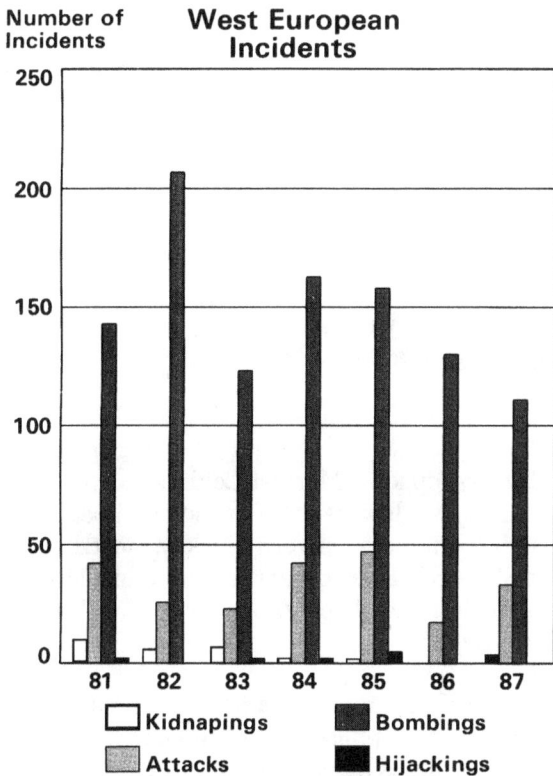

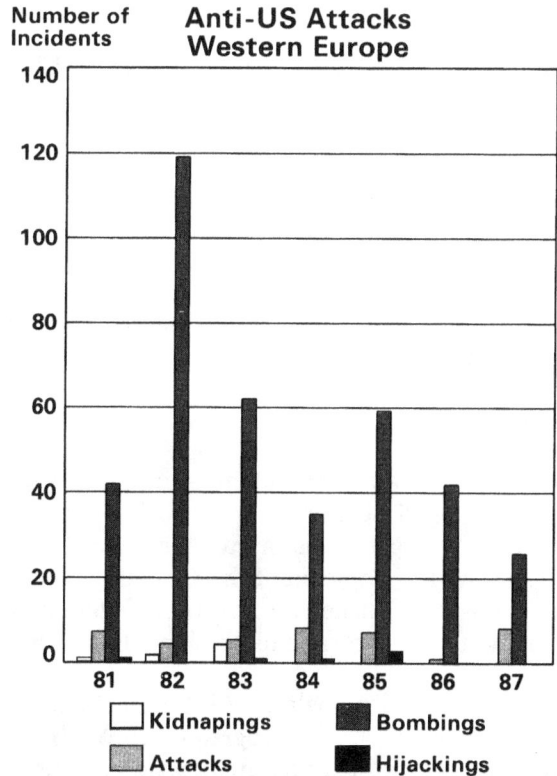

Number of Incidents

West European Incidents

250
200
150
100
50
0

81 82 83 84 85 86 87

☐ Kidnapings   ■ Bombings
▨ Attacks   ■ Hijackings

Number of Incidents

Anti-US Attacks Western Europe

140
120
100
80
60
40
20
0

81 82 83 84 85 86 87

☐ Kidnapings   ■ Bombings
▨ Attacks   ■ Hijackings

are usually from the middle class and are not the deprived members of society more commonly found among rank and file members in the Middle East, Asia, and Latin America. Members are often very well educated and sometimes include doctors, lawyers, and other professionals.

"Ethnic separatists" form another major category of West European terrorism. Examples include Armenians, who almost always target representatives of the Turkish Government and its interests outside Turkey, and Basques, who attack French and Spanish interests inside Spain.

Armenian Secret Army for the Liberation of Armenia (ASALA)

Date Formed 1975.

Estimated Membership Unknown.

Headquarters Unknown.

Area of Operations Worldwide.

Leadership ASALA-RM: Monte Melkonian.
ASALA-M: Hagop Hagopian was leader; killed in March 1988.

Other Names ASALA — Revolutionary Movement (ASALA-RM).
ASALA — Militant (ASALA-M).

Sponsors Suspected relationships with Palestinian radical group Abu Nidal Organization, Kurdish separatist groups, and Syria.

Political Objectives/Target Audiences
- Use revolutionary violence to force an end to the "exploitation, repression, and terror of Turkish colonialism" and the "imperialism" of NATO and Zionism.
- Attack Turkish representatives and institutions anywhere in the world, as well as those of countries that support Turkey.
- Affirm "scientific socialism" as the political doctrine of the reconstituted Armenian homeland.
- Transform Soviet Armenia into a base for revolutionary struggle against Turkey.

Background

ASALA is a transnational, ethnic terrorist organization that espouses a Marxist-Leninist political ideology and solidarity with leftist and separatist movements worldwide. Its principal goal is reestablishing the historical Armenian homeland, an area that includes eastern Turkey, northern Iran, and the Armenian Soviet Socialist Republic of the USSR. ASALA also demands an admission of guilt from Turkey for the alleged genocide of Armenians during the Ottoman Empire, as well as an end to the discrimination they claim Armenians suffer in Turkey.

To further its goals ASALA has committed a series of assassinations, bombings, and assaults. ASALA terrorism has progressed through two phases. During the first phase, the group carried out attacks against Turkish diplomatic personnel and installations to focus attention on the "Armenian question" and gain support among Armenians. In the second phase, ASALA expanded its operations to include attacks against "imperialist" targets. The first of these were bombings in November 1979

Masthead of ASALA's official publication Armenia.

against the KLM and Lufthansa offices in Paris and TWA's office in Madrid. In addition, the group launched attacks against the citizens and property of countries holding ASALA members in prison.

The policy of indiscriminate violence and disputes over leadership eventually caused a split in ASALA. Following the July 1983 ASALA bombing of the Turkish airlines ticket counter at Orly Airport in Paris that killed seven, a dissident group, ASALA-RM, was formed. ASALA-RM views indiscriminate "blind" terrorism as detrimental to the Armenian cause and favors limiting attacks to Turkish targets. ASALA-M continues to favor unrestricted terrorism against Turkish and "imperialist" targets.

Since the split, ASALA's members apparently have been preoccupied with an internal power struggle, leading to a reduction in terrorist activity. ASALA, however, was reported to have been among those involved in a series of bombings in Paris during September 1986 that killed and injured some 200. The attacks were claimed by the Committee for Solidarity with Arab and Middle Eastern Prisoners and were designed to pressure the French Government to release three terrorist prisoners, including ASALA member Varoujan Garabedjian. ALASA has continued to issue threats against French interests to force his release.

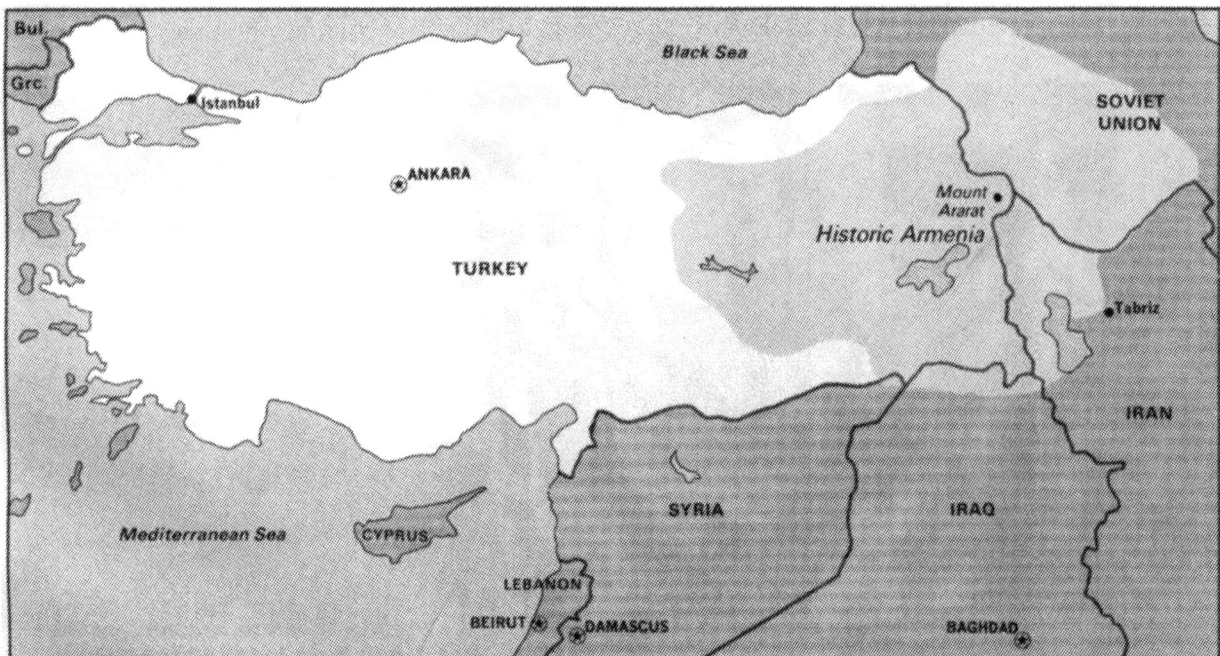

Historic area claimed by Armenian terrorists.

Selected Incident Chronology

January 1975 — Bombed Beirut headquarters of World Council of Churches because of its role in helping Armenians to emigrate to other countries.

February 1976 — Assassinated the First Secretary of the Turkish Embassy in Beirut.

October 1978 — Exploded two bombs in Istanbul, killing one and injuring four.

November 1979 — Bombed the TWA office in Madrid.

December 1979 — Bombed the Turkish airlines office in London. In claiming responsibility, ASALA expressed solidarity with the revolutionary movements in Northern Ireland in their fight against "British fascism."

March 1980 — Bombed the Turkish airlines and Tourist Bureau offices in Rome, killing two, including an American.

January 1981 — Bombed the Swissair office and the Swiss Consulate in Milan in retaliation for the arrest of two Armenian militants in Geneva.

March 1981 — Assassinated the Turkish Labor Attache and Consul for Religious Affairs in Paris.

September 1981 — Stormed the Turkish Consulate in Paris, killing a security guard and seriously wounding a Vice-Consul. The terrorists held 51 persons hostage for 15 hours before surrendering.

June 1982 — Attempted to bomb the Air Canada freight office at Los Angeles International Airport. Police defused the bomb 15 minutes before it was set to explode.

August 1982 — Attacked Ankara's Esenboga Airport, killing 7, including an American, and injuring 72.

An Armenian "suicide" squad killed 7 and wounded over 70 in a 2-hour shooting assault at Turkey's Ankara airport in August 1982.

June 1983 — Carried out a grenade and machinegun attack on the Istanbul bazaar, killing two.

July 1983 — Bombed the Turkish airlines counter at Orly Airport in Paris, killing 7 and injuring over 60.

March 1984 — Shot and injured the First Secretary and the Deputy Military Attache assigned to the Turkish Embassy in Tehran.

January-May 1986 — Staged five incidents in Lebanon, resulting in one kidnaping, nine assassinations, two injuries, and property damage from bombings against Dashnag (Right Wing) Armenian political party members. ASALA claimed involvement or was suspected in all.

September 1986 — Suspected of involvement in the Paris bombing campaign that killed 11 and injured approximately 200.

October 1987 — In East Beirut, Lebanon, gunmen attacked three members of the French Embassy guard force, killing two soldiers and wounding one. ASALA claimed the attack was conducted to put pressure on the French Government to release ASALA prisoners held in France.

Basque Fatherland and Liberty (ETA)

Date Formed 1959.

Estimated Membership Approximately 200 active members.

Headquarters Basque provinces of Spain: Vizcaya, Alava, Guipuzcoa, Navarra; and Basque provinces of France.

Area of Operations Spain and France.

Leadership Jose Antonio Urruticoechea Bengoechea ("Jose Ternera"), Francisco Mugica Garmendia ("Artapalo," "Paquito"), Santiago Arrospide Sarasola ("Santi Potros," captured in France in 1987), Javier Maria or Francisco Javier Larreategui Cuadro ("Atxulo"), Jose Javier Zabaleta Elosegui ("Waldo"), and Eloy Uriarte Diaz de Gereno ("Senor Robles," "El Robles").

Other Names *Euzkadi ta Askatasuna* (original language).

Sponsors None confirmed.

Jose Antonio Urruticoechea Bengoechea, one of the leaders of the Euzkadi ta Askatasuna Militar (ETA-M).

Political Objectives/Target Audiences
- Establish an independent and probably Marxist Basque nation, *Euzkadi,* through terrorism against Spanish interests to pressure the Government of Spain into making desired concessions.
- Create an economic crisis in the Basque provinces by terrorizing businesses in the region.

Background

The ETA is one of the oldest West European terrorist groups currently operating. Although the leadership of the ETA generally espouses a Marxist-Leninist ideology, the primary motivation for many of its members is Basque nationalism.

The ETA actually is composed of several factions that established a loose alliance but still maintain separate identities. The more vehemently aggressive faction is known as the ETA — Military Wing (ETA-M). It advocates a relentless campaign of terrorist violence directed at the Spanish Government. Another faction, the ETA — Political-Military Front (ETA-PM), now largely inactive, pursued a course of terrorism but tried to blend it with grassroots political agitation to broaden the base of revolution. The ETA-M does have political connections through the Herri Batasuna (HB) political party.

The ETA regularly targets Spanish Government officials, members of the military and security forces, and moderate Basques for assassination. In addition, the group has carried out numerous bombings against Government facilities and economic targets, including seasonal campaigns against tourist resorts. The ETA is believed to be responsible for over 500 deaths since 1968, and can claim to be one of the most violent groups in Europe. Funds for ETA terror are generated by kidnapings, armed robberies, and extortion of "revolutionary taxes." Millions of dollars have been "liberated" through large ransoms and bank robberies. The ETA has, on occasion, obtained ransoms of more than $1 million.

The organizational structure of ETA is very sophisticated. The majority of the members (commandos) are organized into three- or four-member cells. Most commandos are "legal" — ETA members, not known to the police, who live open lives without suspicion. They carry out operations and then disappear into their surroundings. A smaller number of commandos are "illegals," who are known to the authorities and live and operate entirely underground. There is also a large group that provides information, communications, and the other support needed to maintain ETA's infrastructure. Resources for a wide-ranging program of terrorism are available not only in the Spanish Basque provinces, but in the French Basque areas along the border, although recent actions by the French Government may have the effect of denying sanctuary there.

The international connections of the ETA are quite extensive. It has reported ties with the Provisional Irish Republican Army, with which it has numerous common characteristics. Its other connections may be based on a common Marxist orientation. In the past ETA members have trained at Middle Eastern terrorist training camps. The Cuban Government has provided safehaven and training for ETA militants. There are also ETA members in Nicaragua, some of whom have been implicated in attacks against opponents of the Sandinista Government. Most of the ETA presence in the region results from transfer agreements between the Spanish Government and the government of the receiving country. Thus, activity associated with ETA members probably involves individuals acting on their own rather than being directed by ETA leaders in Europe.

In fall 1987, a series of complementary arrests in France and Spain resulted from documentation seized by the French during the October 1987 capture of "Santi Potros." Police operations against the ETA have been continuous and often successful. Nonetheless, the ETA seems able to rebound from even the most successful counterterrorist operations. Because of the large size of the group's support base and the high level of nationalist sentiment among the Basques, ETA violence is expected to continue to plague Spain for the foreseeable future.

Selected Incident Chronology

December 1973 — Assassinated Spanish Prime Minister Luis Carrero Blanco, his chauffeur, and a security officer with a remote-controlled bomb.

September 1974 — Bombed a crowded cafe next to a security headquarters in Madrid. Thirteen civilians were killed and 70 were wounded.

October 1976 — Assassinated a senior adviser to King Juan Carlos, his driver, and three security guards. (ETA-M)

March 1978 — Exploded a powerful bomb at the Bilbao nuclear powerplant, killing 2 and wounding 14.

June-July 1979 — Initiated a "tourist war" in the Spanish seaside resort areas. Fourteen time bombs were detonated, injuring 2 and causing extensive property damage. (ETA-PM)

November 1979 — Kidnaped a member of Parliament in Madrid. The victim was released after the Government agreed to review and expedite cases against Basque prisoners and to investigate allegations of torture. (ETA-PM)

February 1980 — Fired an antitank rocket at the Prime Minister's residence in Madrid. The rocket missed the building; there were no injuries. (ETA-PM)

January 1981 — Kidnaped one of the wealthiest men in Spain and held him for 58 days before receiving $3.29 million in ransom. (ETA-PM)

January 1982 — Kidnaped a leading industrialist and held him for a month before receiving a $1.3 million ransom.

October 1982 — Exploded nearly two dozen bombs at several banks in Basque provinces.

February 1983 — Killed three and wounded nine in the bombing of a Bilbao bank that refused to pay "revolutionary taxes."

April 1984 — Killed a retired military officer in Pamplona. A boobytrap in the getaway car exploded when examined, killing two policemen. (ETA-M)

December 1984 — Bombed sections of the Rota-Zaragoza military petroleum pipeline. Claimed the attack was against the Spanish military.

July 1985 — Shot and killed Spain's Director of Defense Policy and seriously wounded his chauffeur in Madrid. (ETA-M)

September 1985 — Exploded a car bomb by remote control, injuring 10 Civil Guardsmen in Madrid. An American in the area was killed. (ETA-M)

February 1986 — Killed Vice Admiral Cristobol Colon and his chauffeur in Madrid in a grenade and gunfire attack. (ETA-M)

July 1986 — Detonated a bomb hidden in a parked van by remote control in Madrid. The 100-pound bomb exploded as a bus carrying Civil Guard Cadets was passing by, killing 10 cadets and injuring several dozen. (ETA-M)

July 1986 — Exploded a bomb in Madrid, Spain, killing nine people.

July 1986 — Fired a dozen antitank rockets by remote control from a homemade launcher at the Ministry of Defense in Madrid, injuring two military officers. After the attack, the car to which the launcher was attached exploded, injuring an additional 10 people. (ETA-M)

October 1986 — Killed General Garido, Governor of Guipuzcoa Province, by placing plastic explosives on the roof of his car. (ETA-M)

December 1986 — Kidnaped a Spanish businessman and held him for 69 days before receiving a $1.5 million ransom. (ETA-M)

January 1987 — Exploded a car bomb, destroying a passing military bus in Zargoza, killing an Army officer and civilian driver and injuring 40.

ETA terrorists bombed this bus in Madrid, Spain, in July 1986, killing 10 people and injuring dozens.

This July 1986 bombing by the ETA killed nine people in Madrid, Spain.

An October 1986 car bombing by Basque terrorists in San Sebastian, Spain, demolished General Garido's vehicle.

General Garido, his wife, and his children were all killed when the car they were in was destroyed by an ETA bomb.

January-February 1987 — Committed a series of arson and bomb attacks against French interests in Mondragon, Bilbao, and Lasarte. One person accidently killed; no other injuries. Believed to be in protest of France's deportation of Basque guerrillas to Spain.

March 1987 — Staged machinegun attack in Vitoria, seriously wounding an Army officer.

March 1987 — Ambushed and wounded an Army officer in Pamplona.

March 1987 — Exploded a bomb at the Barcelona port entrance. One Civil Guardsman was killed and 15 persons injured; extensive property damage.

March-April 1987 — Continued arson and bomb attacks aimed mainly at French property in Ordizia, Barcelona, and Pamplona.

April 1987 — Exploded a car bomb near a Barcelona Civil Guard barracks, killing one and injuring seven.

April 1987 — Police in Burlada found and defused a large, boobytrapped bomb at a sports stadium. It would have caused many casualties if exploded.

May 1987 — Exploded three car bombs near Madrid headquarters of Spanish Navy, Air Force, and Civil Guard, killing one and injuring nine.

May 1987 — Kidnaped a Basque industrialist and held him for 45 days; released after payment of an estimated $1.6 million ransom.

June 1987 — In San Sebastian, exploded a car bomb as two police vans passed; six injured.

June 1987 — Exploded two amonal bombs at a state-owned petrochemical plant. Estimates of damage vary from $8 to $16 million.

June 1987 — Exploded a car bomb in a parking garage under a supermarket in Barcelona, killing 21 and injuring more than 32.

July 1987 — Exploded two grenades in San Sebastian near the offices of the military governor; six injured.

July 1987 — In Onate, exploded a bomb, killing two Civil Guards and wounding two others as their patrol car passed.

July 1987 — Set off a powerful car bomb in front of a Civil Guard building, wounding 20 persons and causing considerable damage.

July 1987 — Directed three bomb attacks at French property in Durango and Pamplona, causing extensive damage.

August 1987 — Attacked a Civil Guard barracks in Zarauz with rocket-propelled grenades, wounding six.

August 1987 — Exploded a bomb in Vitoria as a National Police vehicle passed; two were killed and one injured.

August 1987 — Exploded a car bomb in Eibar, causing heavy property damage and injuring 13.

September 1987 — Set off a car bomb in San Sebastian as two National Police vans passed. One policeman killed and six people injured.

December 1987 — Exploded a car bomb in front of a Spanish Civil Guard apartment complex, causing extensive damage, killing 11, and injuring 40.

Combatant Communist Cells (CCC)

Date Formed 1984.

Estimated Membership Unknown.

Headquarters Brussels.

Area of Operations Belgium.

Leadership Pierre Carrette.

Other Names *Cellules Communistes Combattantes* (original language).

Sponsors None known.

Pierre Carette, suspected leader of the Combatant Communist Cells.

Political Objectives/Target Audiences
- Destroy the capitalist system and oppose "imperialist wars."
- Destroy NATO.
- Use terrorism to force a reversal of Belgium's defense and economic policies in the short run and foster socialist revolution thereafter.

Background

The CCC literally exploded onto the European terrorism stage with a series of bombings that began in October 1984 and ended in December 1985 with the police apprehension of its leader and three other militants. The origins of this Marxist-Leninist terrorist group appear to lie in the Belgian political dissent in the early 1980s over defense, economic, ethnic, and environmental policies. Impatience with the Government's inability to resolve these problems to their liking and the belief that terrorism would mobilize leftist opponents of the Government and precipitate its downfall helped lead radical leftists to form the CCC.

Prior to the CCC's emergence, Belgium had not been troubled by an indigenous terrorist threat. Throughout the 1970s, however, Belgium was a refuge for European terrorists fleeing their own countries. The alleged founder and now imprisoned leader of the CCC, Pierre Carrette (a long-time militant in Belgian ultraleft political circles), had contacts with terrorists from the French group Direct Action (AD) and the West German Red Army Faction (RAF) prior to the emergence of the CCC in October 1984.

The CCC is believed to have joined with the RAF and AD in forming an Anti-Imperialist Armed Front to conduct attacks to protest the "Americanization of Europe" and to frustrate increased military cooperation among members of NATO. Although the current existence of such an umbrella organization is in doubt, the CCC shares common ideological goals with both the RAF and the AD.

The CCC relied upon bombings as its sole mode of attack during its period of activity. The only fatalities for which it was responsible were the deaths of two firemen during a bombing attack in May 1985. Aside from links with the RAF and the AD, there are no indications of contacts with other terrorist groups or evidence of foreign support for the CCC.

There have been no known CCC attacks since the apprehension of Carrette and the other three militants in December 1985. While police successes appear to have eliminated the CCC threat, it is possible that they have only caused it to halt operations temporarily and to enter a rebuilding phase.

Selected Incident Chronology

October 1984 — Bombed the headquarters of Litton Data Systems in Brussels; 3 buildings and 25 vehicles severely damaged. Also bombed during October the parking lot of the M.A.N. Corporation, the headquarters of Honeywell-Bull, and the Belgian Liberal Party Research Center, all in the Brussels area.

November 1984 — Bombed two telecommunications towers at a NATO airbase near Liege.

December 1984 — Simultaneously bombed points along the NATO fuel pipeline, forcing a temporary shutdown of operations.

January 1985 — Injured two American military policemen in the bombing of a NATO support facility in suburban Brussels.

May 1985 — Bombed the Belgian Employers Federation building (resulting in the death of two firemen) and the central offices of the Belgian Police General Directorate for Logistics and Finance.

October 1985 — Bombed the headquarters of a Belgian gas company, a Belgian steel company, and the information offices of the Belgian Army.

December 1985 — In Antwerp, Belgium, exploded a bomb at the Bank of America offices. The bomb caused major damage to the building and surrounding area, but only two passersby were injured.

December 1985 — In Versailles, placed a bomb on a windowsill in the rear of a building belonging to Central Europe Operating Agency (CEOA), manager of the network of NATO pipelines in Belgium, France, Luxembourg, the Netherlands, and West Germany. The same day, exploded a bomb at a NATO Central European pipeline valve station near Ghent, Belgium, causing minor damage.

Direct Action (AD)

Date Formed 1979.

Estimated Membership Unknown.

Headquarters Paris, Lyons.

Area of Operations France, Belgium.

Leadership Jean-Marc Rouillan, Nathalie Menigon, Joelle Aubran, Georges Cipriani (all arrested by the French police in February 1987), Regis Schleicher (sentenced to life imprisonment in June 1987), Max Frerot, Frederic Oriach, Andre Olivier (arrested in 1986), Eric Moreau.

Other Names *Accion Directe* (original language).

Sponsors None known.

Political Objectives/Target Audiences
- "Wreck society through direct action by destroying its institutions and the men who serve it, and by relying on the people's forces."
- Further class confrontation between the masses and "Western imperialism."
- Oppose US presence on the Continent, which is viewed as causing the "Americanization" of Europe.
- Carry out attacks in support of "anti-Zionist" causes.

Background

The AD is believed to have evolved from French radical groups of the 1970s such as the Revolutionary International Action Group (GARI) and the Armed Nuclei for Popular Autonomy

(NAPAP). These groups occasionally resorted to terrorist tactics, but never demonstrated the organizational sophistication and operational capability displayed by the AD.

AD's anarchistic orientation has led it to develop a highly decentralized organization in which specific terrorist acts are planned and conducted by terrorist cells operating in relative isolation. The AD is believed to be divided into two wings, one international and one domestic, with the domestic wing being less violent. The international wing, based in Paris and allegedly Belgium, headed by Rouillon, has perpetrated several sophisticated bombings and assassinations targeting individuals and institutions associated with the military and with West European industry, as well as institutions symbolizing both European cooperation and US-European ties. The domestic wing seems to prefer exclusively French targets and usually bombs unoccupied buildings. The AD has financed its operations primarily through bank robberies and has used a wide variety of weaponry and explosives in its attacks.

The international wing of the AD allied itself with the German Red Army Faction (RAF) and possibly the Belgian Combatant Communist Cells (CCC) to form the Anti-Imperialist Armed Front. This front called for the formation of an "international proletarian urban combat organization" to combat the "Americanization of NATO" and thwart moves toward greater military cooperation within the Atlantic Alliance. The international wing of the AD and the RAF may have conducted joint operations such as the January 1985 assassination of French General Rene Audran and the August 1985 bombing of Rhein Main Air Base. Evidence uncovered in AD safehouses revealed strong logistical and perhaps even operational links between the AD and the RAF.

The AD also is believed to have ties with other West European and Middle Eastern terrorist groups: The AD may have contacts with the Italian Red Brigades. There is evidence the AD provided explosives to the Irish National Liberation Army. The AD also is alleged to have cooperated with the Lebanese Armed Revolutionary Faction on several attacks carried out in France.

The AD has not conducted an attack since the arrest of the international wing's leadership cadre in February 1987. The group is believed to have been severely crippled by police successes in 1986 and 1987.

Selected Incident Chronology

May 1979 — Machinegunned the building of the National Council of French Employers in Paris.

March 1980 — Bombed and completely destroyed the police station in Toulouse.

May 1980 — Injured eight with a bomb at Orly Airport in Paris.

April 1981 — Wounded a policeman in an attack on a Paris bank.

December 1981 — Bombed a toy store, a Rolls Royce dealership, an exclusive restaurant, and a clothes store.

June 1982 — Bombed the American School in Paris and the European headquarters of the World Bank.

August 1982 — Machinegunned an empty Israeli Embassy auto, and bombed a Jewish-owned hardware store and bank.

September 1983 — Killed 1 and injured 23 with a bomb at the Marseilles Trade Fair.

November 1983 — Injured one in a church bombing in Paris.

July 1984 — Claimed responsibility for the bombing of the Industry Ministry in Paris.

The French-based Direct Action claimed responsibility for this July 1984 bombing of the Industry Ministry in Paris.

August 1984 — Wounded seven in the bombing of the European Space Agency.

January 1985 — Murdered French General Rene Audran, shooting him eight times (apparently a joint operation with the German Red Army Faction).

June 1985 — Attempted to kill General Henri Blandin, Comptroller General of the Armed Forces, in Paris.

April 1986 — Attempted to murder Guy Brana, vice president of the French Employers' Union.

May 1986 — Believed to have been responsible for bombing the headquarters of Interpol in suburban Paris.

July 1986 — Claimed responsibility for bombing the offices of the special anticrime squad of the French Judicial Police in Paris.

July 1986 — Employed a car bomb against the Paris headquarters of the Organization for Economic Cooperation and Development.

November 1986 — Murdered Georges Besse, Chairman of Renault, with gunfire.

November 1986 — Bombed the National Immigration offices in Paris.

December 1986 — Killed a chauffeur while attempting to assassinate former Justice Minister Alain Peyrefitte with a bomb attached to his car.

January 1987 — Planted a grenade near the Paris apartment of the judge presiding over the Schleicher trial; it was discovered and disarmed.

The National Immigration offices in Paris after they were bombed by France's Direct Action, in November 1986.

First of October Anti-Fascist Resistance Group (GRAPO)

Date Formed 1975.

Estimated Membership Probably less than 25.

Area of Operations Spain.

Leadership Manuel Perez Martinez ("Camarada Arenas").

Other Names *Grupo de Resistencia Antifascista, Primero de Octubre* (original language).

Sponsors None known.

Political Objectives/Target Audiences
- Violently overthrow the Spanish Government and establish a Marxist state.
- Oppose Spain's participation in NATO and US presence in Spain.

Background

The GRAPO was established as the "military" arm of the outlawed Communist Party of Spain — Reconstituted (PCE-R), which is a splinter group of the official and recognized Communist Party of Spain (PCE). An urban-oriented group, GRAPO has committed assassinations, bombings, and kidnapings against Spanish personnel and facilities. On occasion it also has attacked US interests. The group has preferred ambushes using automatic weapons.

Like the ETA, the other major Spanish terrorist group, the GRAPO has financed its operations through kidnap ransoms, bank robberies, and extorting "revolutionary taxes" from individuals and businesses. These sources of funds have proved adequate for financing its range of operations and for procuring weapons and explosives.

Direct ties between the GRAPO and foreign terrorist groups or state sponsors have not been established. The GRAPO, however, has made public statements in support of a number of other terrorist groups, including the German Red Army Faction and the Italian Red Brigades.

GRAPO's structure has been based on a cellular concept for maximum internal security. These cells are probably quite small in view of the group's limited numbers. GRAPO members are either "legal commandos" or "liberated commandos." The legal commandos, unknown to police, lead apparently normal lives and periodically carry out terrorist actions. The liberated commandos are full-time members who are known to the authorities and live underground.

Successful Spanish police operations led to the arrests of the most significant known GRAPO members in January 1985. Although the GRAPO has not committed any significant act of terrorism since December 1984, it has demonstrated the capability to rebuild and to conduct minor operations, such as the robberies that took place in southern Spain in 1987.

Selected Incident Chronology

January 1977 — Kidnaped the president of the Supreme Military Tribunal and former Army Chief of Staff. He was rescued in a police raid the next month.

May 1977 — Bombed the US Cultural Center in Madrid on the day Vice President Mondale arrived for an official visit.

March 1978 — Assassinated the Director of Penal Institutions in Madrid.

March 1979 — Assassinated a semiretired Spanish brigadier general in Madrid and claimed it was a protest of Spain's pending entry into NATO.

May 1979 — Killed 8 and wounded 40 with a bomb blast at a Madrid cafe frequented by rightists.

September 1980 — Killed a general and wounded his aide and driver by machinegun fire, in Barcelona.

April 1982 — Ambushed two policemen in Barcelona, killing one and wounding the other.

August 1982 — Exploded bombs at the Bank of America in Madrid and at a Sears building in Barcelona.

May 1983 — Shot and killed a Civil Guardsman in a school bus in La Coruna, northern Spain.

January 1984 — Shot and killed two policemen in Madrid.

April 1984 — Kidnaped a bank official and released him after a large ransom was paid.

May 1984 — Exploded a series of bombs at Government offices in Madrid, Barcelona, and other cities.

July 1984 — Robbed the French Bank Credit Lyonnais, in Barcelona, of 300,000 pesetas (approximately $1,800). Gunmen set off a bomb that completely destroyed the bank and injured one person.

July-August 1984 — Exploded a series of 15 bombs in several cities, causing extensive property damage to a French bank, a French Consulate, and the US General Motors Company, among others. No injuries sustained.

September 1984 — Murdered the president of the Seville Association of Businessmen.

September 1984 — In Madrid, killed the director general of a large real estate company.

September 1984 — In La Coruna, severely wounded a radio engineer in a machinegun attack.

September 1984 — Kidnaped the director general of a company, who was forced to write a bank draft for about $30,000. A company employee then was kidnaped and made to cash the draft. The two were released and the gunmen escaped.

December 1984 — Carried out three successful kidnapings, and took only a few hours to receive ransoms of $11,000 to $17,000. Victims released.

February 1986 — Took four hostages in a failed bank robbery attempt. Robbers captured and hostages released.

July 1987 — Fired shots at and severely injured a national policeman who was on watch in front of a police station.

Iraultza

Date Formed 1982.

Estimated Membership Less than 20.

Headquarters Unknown.

Area of Operations Basque provinces of Spain: Vizcaya, Alava, Guipuzcoa, and Navarra.

Leadership Unknown.

Other Names Basque Armed Revolutionary Worker's Organization.

Sponsors None known.

Political Objectives/Target Audiences
- Establish an independent, Marxist Basque nation.
- End foreign investment in the Basque region.
- Protest US foreign policy, particularly in Latin America.

Background

Little is known about the Basque terrorist group Iraultza, and its origins are obscure. Marxist and strongly anti-US, Iraultza seeks to establish an independent, Marxist Basque nation and to end foreign, particularly US, investment in the Basque region. In addition, the group opposes US foreign policy, particularly toward Latin America, expressing solidarity with radical leftists there.

Although Iraultza is believed to consist of fewer than 20 members, it has committed numerous bombings against US and French economic interests in the Basque region. The group has probably committed more bombings against US business interests than any other European terrorist group, causing thousands of dollars in damage. Anonymous callers claiming responsibility for Iraultza bombings (written communiques are not known to exist) have voiced opposition to US aid to the Nicaraguan resistance, US actions in Grenada and Lebanon, and Spain's participation in NATO. Attacks against French interests have been prompted by the arrest and expulsion of Basque terrorists from France. Iraultza, however, has not directly attacked US Government personnel or facilities.

Operating in the Spanish provinces of Vizcaya, Alava, Guipuzcoa, and Navarra, Iraultza seeks to establish an independent, Marxist Basque nation.

Iraultza members leave small, unsophisticated bombs on the sidewalk or in the street outside the intended target, late at night. Although an anonymous caller then warns the police, there is usually not enough time for the police to react before the bomb explodes. Intending only to cause property damage, Iraultza's "midnight" bombs have injured several people and killed a construction worker when one of its bombs malfunctioned.

There is no information available on Iraultza's leadership, organization, or source of funding. Since the group is quite small and its bombs are simple, Iraultza likely survives on money and equipment provided by supporters and through petty extortion. Although currently considered a minor group, Iraultza has the potential to be a more serious threat.

Selected Incident Chronology

May 1982 — Bombed the stock market and a bank in Bilbao. There were no injuries.

February 1983 — Claimed responsibility for an attempted bombing of the Rank Xerox offices in Bilbao. Police defused the bomb.

April 1983 — Bombed the Rank Xerox office in Pamplona. There were no injuries.

May 1983 — Bombed three banks in the Basque province of Guipuzcoa, causing $225,000 in damages but no injuries.

May 1983 — Bombed the Rank Xerox office in Bilbao. There were no injuries.

June 1983 — Bombed a General Motors-affiliated company in San Sebastian to protest US investment in the Basque region and a visit by the Spanish Prime Minister to Washington. There were no injuries.

November 1983 — Bombed the Bilbao offices of the Bank of America and Rank Xerox in protest of the US actions in Grenada and the presence of US Marines in Lebanon. There were no injuries.

November 1983 — Bombed the Coca Cola bottling plant in San Sebastian, causing considerable damage but no injuries.

December 1983 — Bombed the IBM office in Vitoria, the 3M office in Bilbao, and the NCR and Coca Cola offices in San Sebastian. There were no injuries.

December 1983 — Bombed the Hispanoamerican Cultural Center office in Bilbao. There were no injuries. (The center is not affiliated with the United States.)

January 1984 — Bombed a Ford dealership in Bilbao. There were no injuries.

November 1984 — Bombed the IBM offices in Bilbao, causing considerable damage but no injuries.

January 1985 — Bombed a Bilbao movie theater that was showing the American film *Red Dawn*. There were no injuries.

February 1985 — Bombed the Firestone office in Bilbao to commemorate the death of a group member and in "solidarity with the people of Latin America and its struggle against US imperialism." There were no injuries.

May 1985 — Bombed the Hertz and Avis offices in San Sebastian. There were no injuries.

November 1985 — Bombed the offices of Honeywell Bull in San Sebastian. There were no injuries.

January 1986 — Bombed the offices of Rank Xerox in Bilbao. There were no injuries.

February 1986 — Bombed the Vitoria office of Citibank in "behalf of the anti-NATO movement." There were no injuries.

June 1986 — Bombed the offices of the 3M Company in Bilbao to protest US aid to the Nicaraguan resistance. There were no injuries.

June 1986 — Bombed a Bilbao construction site to protest the building of a waste treatment plant, killing a worker when the bomb, set to detonate at night, exploded during working hours.

September 1986 — Bombed a bank in Vitoria. There were no injuries.

October 1986 — Suspected in the bombing of five automobile showrooms displaying French cars, slightly injuring three passersby.

March 1987 — Bombed the NCR offices in Bilbao, causing minor damage but no injuries.

March 1988 — In Vitoria, Spain, bombed a Ford showroom, causing considerable damage to the showroom and to nearby parked cars. No injuries were reported.

Irish National Liberation Army (INLA)

Date Formed 1975.

Estimated Membership Less than 20.

Headquarters Dublin.

Area of Operations No significant rural presence in Northern Ireland, but active in urban areas such as Belfast and Londonderry.

Leadership Dominic McGlinchey (killed in 1987), Harry Flynn (arrested in France in 1986), Gerard Steenson (killed in 1987), Thomas Power (killed in 1987).

Other Names None.

Sponsors None Known.

Political Objectives/Target Audiences
- Form a united 32-county Socialist Republic in Ireland.
- Oust the British from Northern Ireland through violence, and overthrow the elected Government of the Republic of Ireland.

Background

The INLA is the military arm of the Irish Republican Socialist Party (IRSP), a political splinter group of the Official Irish Republican Army (OIRA). The late Seamus Costello, the OIRA Adjutant General, was expelled from the OIRA in 1974 and that same year, with other OIRA dissidents, founded the IRSP. The IRSP denies its connection with the INLA, but its newspaper, *The Starry Plough*, reports INLA military operations, and the relationship between the two groups is clear. The INLA is widely regarded as more Marxist in orientation than the Provisional Irish Republican Army (PIRA).

In the first few years following its creation, the INLA feuded with both wings (the OIRA and the PIRA) of the Irish Replication Army. Many militants were killed, including the IRSP's founder Seamus Costello, who was gunned down in 1977. Despite ideological and tactical differences, the

INLA has collaborated with the PIRA. At one time, this cooperation reportedly involved regular weekly meetings. Occasional friction between the groups continues to occur, but their differences no longer erupt into the bloody killing seen in the mid-1970s.

Although the INLA has engaged in bombings and shootings since 1975, it achieved widespread notoriety only after the March 1979 assassination of leading British Conservative Party member Airey Neave in Great Britain. This INLA action shocked British authorities. The attack was noteworthy because it represented an expansion of INLA activities outside of Ireland, and it used a sophisticated explosive device.

In Northern Ireland, typical INLA operations include bombings and shootings, targeting British soldiers, members of Northern Ireland's security forces, Ulster government officials, and members of loyalist political parties and paramilitary groups. The INLA has used a wide variety of handguns, machineguns, and grenades and tends to use commercially available explosives in its bombings.

Bank, payroll, and train robberies both in Ulster and the Republic of Ireland appear to be the primary sources of INLA funding. The group apparently does not have the access to the international funding enjoyed by the PIRA and may have begun to resort to extortion to meet operational expenses.

There is evidence of INLA contacts with the West German Revolutionary Cells (RZ) and the French Direct Action (AD). RZ and INLA militants reportedly have exchanged visits. British sources claim that the explosives to have been used in INLA's aborted 1985 plot to bomb the Chelsea Barracks in London were stolen by AD members in France in 1984. In accordance with its Marxist ideology, the INLA also has expressed solidarity with numerous national liberation and terrorist movements throughout the world.

Numerous arrests of INLA terrorists and testimony by "supergrass" informers (INLA and PIRA militants who inform on their former comrades) have reduced INLA operational capabilities significantly and caused the group to limit its activities. Problems in permitting the use of "supergrass" testimony in court, however, led to the release in 1987 of many captured INLA militants. Upon their release, a bloody feud erupted over whether to disband the organization, and many militants were killed. Despite this preoccupation with internal leadership conflicts, the INLA remains a brutal and unpredictable organization.

Selected Incident Chronology

March 1979 — Assassinated Airey Neave, British Conservative Party member and spokesman on Northern Ireland, with a car bomb.

November 1979 — Bombed the British Consulate in Antwerp, Belgium.

April 1981 — Attempted to assassinate Kenneth Shimeld, Permanent Secretary of the Northern Ireland Office, with a boobytrap bomb.

December 1982 — Bombed a crowded nightclub frequented by British soldiers in Ballykelly; 17 people were killed, 12 of them soldiers, and 66 were wounded.

November 1983 — Fired into the congregation of the Mountain Lodge Gospel Hall in Dardley. Three people were killed and seven were injured.

March 1985 — Exploded a car bomb near the Belfast site of an England-Northern Ireland soccer match. Police were alerted ahead of time and no injuries resulted.

September 1986 — Placed a 50-pound bomb outside the British Legion Hall in County Down; it was defused by British Army personnel.

January 1987 — Attempted to assassinate David Calvert, a prominent Unionist politician in Northern Ireland.

January-June 1987 — At least six persons were murdered and three injured in internal power struggles among factions of the INLA.

Justice Commandos of the Armenian Genocide (JCAG)

Date Formed 1975.

Estimated Membership Unknown.

Headquarters Unknown.

Area of Operations Worldwide.

Leadership Unknown.

Other Names Armenian Revolutionary Army (ARA).

Sponsors None known outside of the international Armenian community.

Political Objectives/Target Audiences
- Reestablish the Independent Republic of Armenia that existed briefly in eastern Turkey after World War I.
- Seek an admission of guilt and the payment of reparations by Turkey for the alleged genocide of Armenians during the Ottoman Empire.
- Direct the struggle for an Armenian homeland through attacks on the Turkish Government.
- Paralyze Turkish diplomacy by striking at its highest levels.
- Disrupt the Turkish economy through attacks on Government-owned enterprises and prevent international economic assistance to Turkey.

Background

Unlike its Marxist rival, the Armenian Secret Army for the Liberation of Armenia (ASALA), the JCAG does not seek reunification with the Armenian Soviet Socialist Republic in the USSR. The JCAG's vision for a future Armenian government is similar to European social democratic political systems.

Drawing on elements from the large Armenian communities abroad for support, the JCAG has committed a series of assassinations and bombings against official Turkish personnel and facilities worldwide. JCAG operations usually favor ambushes of Turkish officials in or near their automobiles or bombings of Turkish facilities. In the belief that Western public opinion is too valuable to its cause to risk alienation through indiscriminate violence, the JCAG has limited its attacks to Turkish targets. Despite these "intentions," other nationalities have been victims of JCAG terrorism.

Little is known about the JCAG's leadership, organization, or ties to other groups. Although the JCAG has expressed solidarity with other movements such as the Basque ETA and Turkish Kurds, whether the JCAG maintains operational ties with other groups is not known.

Around 1983, a group called the Armenian Revolutionary Army (ARA) began claiming responsibility for anti-Turkish attacks and JCAG fell from use. Similarities to past JCAG attacks may indicate that ARA is a covername for JCAG.

Selected Incident Chronology

October 1975 — Assassinated the Turkish Ambassador to Austria in his Vienna office. Incident also was claimed by ASALA.

October 1975 — Assassinated the Turkish Ambassador to France as his car was tied up in Paris traffic.

May 1976 — Bombed the Turkish Consulate and the Turkish Garanzi Bank in Zurich.

June 1977 — Assassinated the Turkish Ambassador to the Vatican City.

June 1978 — Killed the wife, brother-in-law, and chauffeur of the Turkish Ambassador to Spain as their car was held up in Madrid traffic.

July 1979 — Bombed the offices of the Turkish airlines, the Turkish Tourist Bureau, and the Labor Attache in Paris.

December 1979 — Killed the head of the Turkish Tourist Bureau in Paris.

February 1980 — Wounded the Turkish Ambassador to Switzerland.

October 1980 — Claimed responsibility for bombings in New York and Los Angeles. A car containing six sticks of dynamite exploded outside Turkey's United Nations mission in New York, injuring five people. In Los Angeles, a passerby was injured when a bomb damaged the travel agency owned by a man of Turkish descent.

December 1980 — Assassinated the Turkish Consul General and his bodyguard in Sydney, Australia.

January 1982 — Assassinated the Turkish Consul General in Los Angeles as he drove to his office.

May 1982 — Assassinated the Turkish Honorary Consul in Boston as he drove home.

June 1982 — Assassinated the Turkish Commercial Attache and his wife as they parked their car in Lisbon.

August 1982 — Assassinated the Turkish Military Attache in Ottawa.

March 1983 — Assassinated the Turkish Ambassador to Yugoslavia while his auto was stopped for a red light in Belgrade. A passerby also was killed, and a Yugoslav policeman was injured.

July 1983 — Seized the Turkish Embassy in Lisbon. Seven people were killed, including the wife of the Charge d'Affaires, a security officer, and the five terrorists. Claimed by the ARA.

June 1984 — Exploded a car bomb in Vienna, killing the Labor Attache of the Turkish Embassy and injuring five. Incident was claimed by the ARA, which emphasized that it targeted only Turkish diplomats.

September 1984 — Killed the Turkish Deputy Director of the UN Center for Social Development and Humanitarian Affairs as his car slowed for a red light in Vienna. Claimed by the ARA.

March 1985 — Seized the Turkish Embassy in Ottawa, killing a Canadian security guard and holding 13 persons hostage before surrendering. Claimed by ARA.

Popular Forces 25 April (FP-25)

Date Formed 1980.

Estimated Membership 6-10 hardcore members and 100-200 sympathizers.

Headquarters Lisbon, Oporto, Barcelos.

Area of Operations Portugal.

Leadership Lieutenant Colonel Otelo Saraiva de Carvalho (currently serving a 15-year sentence after being convicted of leading the group). Information on the current leadership is unavailable.

Other Names *Forces Populares 25 de Abril* (original language), Autonomus Revolutionary Groups (GAR), Armed Revolutionary Organization (ORA).

Sponsors No major foreign sponsors, although Libya reportedly has provided some support.

Political Objectives/Target Audiences
- Achieve the violent overthrow of the Portuguese Government and establish a Marxist state.
- Demonstrate violent opposition to US and NATO presence in Portugal.
- Conduct attacks in Portugal in support of other European terrorist groups.

Background

The stated goals of the FP-25 are "to use armed force against imperialism" and lead a "workers' assault on bourgeois power." The group was named after the 25 April 1974 military coup that ousted the rightwing regime that had ruled Portugal since 1926. It claims to be a workers' organization dedicated to a struggle against exploitation, misery, and repression, as well as to the violent overthrow of the Portuguese Government. The FP-25 also is virulently anti-US and anti-NATO. The group has committed a series of assassinations, bombings, and rocket attacks against Portuguese Government and economic targets. In addition, the group has targeted the interests of the United States and the NATO Alliance in Portugal.

Few details concerning the organizational structure of the FP-25 are known. In an interview given to a Portuguese Communist Party journalist in 1984, two men who claimed to be FP-25 members said the group's structure was cellular and placed a high degree of emphasis on security. Reportedly, only armed militants are allowed to assume leadership positions. Support elements are kept at arm's length to minimize infiltration by the police.

There is no evidence of extensive foreign support for the FP-25. Press reports have claimed that Portuguese authorities are aware of some financial support from Libya. There also is no evidence of direct ties to other European terrorist groups despite the fact that the FP-25 has conducted acts of terrorism directed at US, British, French, and West German targets to express solidarity with various groups. In recent years the FP-25 has chosen to focus more of its energy on attacking US and NATO targets.

The FP-25's capabilities were damaged by a series of Portuguese counterterrorist successes, including the arrest of 56 members in 1984. It is possible that the group is reorganizing after being in disarray.

Selected Incident Chronology

May 1980 — Killed a guard outside the home of the Minister of Finance in an abortive kidnaping attempt.

May 1980 — Killed a Portuguese businessman after failing in efforts to extort money from him.

May 1980 — Bombed the British Airways office in Oporto and rocketed the Royal Club in Lisbon as a show of support for the Provisional Irish Republican Army.

December 1982 — Killed the head of a porcelain factory near Lisbon. He was accused of repressive actions against the working class.

November-December 1983 — Over a 6-week period, detonated a series of bombs around Lisbon to protest labor policies. There were several injuries.

February 1984 — Robbed an armored car transporting over $800,000 in Lisbon.

October 1984 — Attempted to fire two antitank rockets at the US Embassy in Lisbon. The attack failed when the terrorists accidentally damaged the firing circuit of the rockets during loading.

November 1984 — Fired four mortar rounds at the US Embassy compound, damaging two vehicles.

December 1984 — Fired four mortar rounds at NATO's Iberian Atlantic Command Headquarters near Lisbon, damaging a car and several buildings.

January 1985 — Fired three mortar rounds at NATO ships anchored in Lisbon harbor. None were hit.

February 1985 — Detonated eight incendiary bombs under cars belonging to West Germany Air Force personnel assigned to a Portuguese airbase outside Beja. The explosions injured one person and caused considerable damage.

July 1985 — Fatally shot the key prosecution witness, a former group member, before he could testify at a major trial of suspected FP-25 members.

September 1985 — Engineered the escape of 10 FP-25 members held in a Lisbon jail.

February 1986 — Assassinated the Director General of the National Prison System in Lisbon.

May 1986 — Fired a mortar round at the headquarters of NATO's Iberian Atlantic Command. There were no injuries or damage.

September 1986 — Bombed several tourist resorts in Southern Portugal. There were no injuries. The bombings were claimed by the Armed Revolutionary Organization (ORA) — probably a FP-25 covername.

Provisional Irish Republican Army (PIRA)

Date Formed 1970.

Estimated Membership 200-400 hardcore.

Headquarters Northern Ireland, Irish Republic.

Area of Operations Primarily Northern Ireland, occasionally England and continental Europe.

Leadership Gerry Adams, Martin McGuiness.

Other Names Provos.

Sponsors Libya.

Political Objectives/Target Audiences
- Establish a unified Ireland under a "Socialist" government.
- Undermine British support for Northern Ireland remaining in the United Kingdom through a campaign of attrition and terrorism.
- Convince the international Irish community to support the PIRA.

Background

Since Northern Ireland separated from the Irish Republic when the latter gained its independence in 1921, the Roman Catholic minority in Northern Ireland has protested discrimination by the Protestant-controlled Government and has agitated for unification in both violent and nonviolent campaigns. In the late 1960s, a strong Catholic civil rights campaign emerged that featured confrontational politics and occasional violent protests. In 1969, the dormant Irish Republican Army split into two wings — Official (OIRA) and Provisional (PIRA). Initially both wings were aggressively militant, but in 1972, the Officials became nonviolent. Other Northern Irish extremist groups emerged, but the PIRA has maintained its leading position.

Most PIRA adherents, particularly in the rural areas, are traditional Irish nationalists, or Republicans, as are older veterans of the movement. Ranged against these conservative forces, however, and at present dominating them, is a group of younger leaders, primarily from Northern Ireland, who have radical leftist tendencies. They sponsored PIRA's dual "Armalite and Ballot Box" strategy, according to which PIRA has pursued terrorism while at the same time promoting the efforts of its political wing, Provisional Sinn Fein, to become a legitimate political force in both Northern Ireland and the Republic of Ireland. Many conservative, traditional PIRA members reportedly are suspicious of the Socialist inclinations and political aspirations of the new leadership. They fear that PIRA will be drawn toward political activity, forsaking violence and terrorism, which in their view are the only effective weapons in the struggle to achieve the group's goals.

PIRA terrorism is designed to move the people of Northern Ireland and Britain to pressure the British Government to withdraw from Northern Ireland and let the Catholic and Protestant Irish settle the conflict without British interference. By using violence, the Provos also hope to focus worldwide attention on the struggle against British "oppression" and thereby generate broader international pressure on the British Government. In 1984-85, some of these people split from the Provisional Sinn Fein, when the latter's annual convention approved more political activity, and formed the "Republican Sinn Fein." PIRA leaders have settled in for a long war of attrition in the hope that the prohibitive economic costs and international stigma attached to Britain's presence in Northern Ireland will drive the British Army out of Ulster, while admitting that a military victory is unlikely.

The PIRA has focused its energy on creating maximum casualties from the beginning. The over 1,000 victims who have died, and a far greater number who have been injured, are grim testimony to the PIRA's determination to "wash the British out of Ireland on a wave of blood." Favored PIRA targets include the British Army, Ulster security forces, prison and judicial officials, and Loyalist political party members. Most attacks have occurred in Northern Ireland, but occasionally actions have been carried out in the Republic of Ireland, Great Britain, and other West European nations. PIRA methods of attack include shootings, bombings, and mortar attacks. The PIRA arsenal is large and varied and is thought to include various handguns, machineguns, grenades, RPG-7 grenade launchers, and a variety of homemade, commercial, and military explosives.

In the early 1970s, the police were especially effective in using information from informers to round up large numbers of PIRA radicals. As a result, beginning in 1977, the PIRA was reorganized. The cells (called Active Service Units — ASUs) are compartmentalized, with members knowing only each other and the person issuing orders from above. They also are functionally specialized in such activities as intelligence, snipings, executions, bombings, or robberies, and are capable of operating outside of their own areas to confuse security forces. The cells are subordinate to local commands or brigades and ultimately responsible to a new "Northern Command," the primary PIRA operational authority.

Beginning in 1982, the British Government succeeded in convincing many former PIRA terrorists to inform on their comrades-in-arms. These informers (referred to as "supergrasses") have helped the British (along with their highly developed surveillance and intelligence methods) to arrest many PIRA militants. Nevertheless, PIRA actions — such as the 1984 bombing at Brighton in an attempt to assassinate British Prime Minister Thatcher and much of her Cabinet — indicate that the group remains a potent force.

Financial support for the PIRA has come from a variety of sources. Its civilian support base is a continuous source. Robberies of banks, post offices, and corporate payrolls also are used routinely. Private US citizens have been a source of funds. The PIRA also has received large amounts of money from the Government of Libya.

In addition to money, the PIRA has received arms and possibly training from Libya. In 1973, 5 tons of Libyan weapons were intercepted off the coast of Ireland. PIRA leader Joe Cahill was aboard the ship. Later the Libyans allegedly gave the PIRA between 1 and 2 million British pounds in financial assistance. This support ended after Protestant approaches to Libya, but was resumed in the early 1980s. In April 1986, the British Secretary of State for Northern Ireland stated publicly that substantial support in arms and cash had been provided to the PIRA by Libya since 1982. In November 1987, a Libyan arms shipment to the PIRA, containing various weapons, ammunition, and explosives, was confiscated off the French coast.

In addition to the Libyan connection, the PIRA is reported to have links with other terrorist organizations. The PIRA's closest ally among European terrorist groups is reported to be the Spanish Basque group Fatherland and Liberty. Close links between these two groups allegedly date back to the early 1970s. The PIRA allegedly also has had contacts with the the West German Revolutionary Cells and appears to have strong support structures in West Germany, the Netherlands, and Belgium.

Selected Incident Chronology

July 1972 — Killed 9 and injured 130 in 19 bombings in Belfast on "Bloody Friday."

September 1973 — Conducted extensive bombings of British targets, including the London Stock Exchange, the House of Commons, the Bank of England, an air terminal, the London subway, and major shopping areas.

February 1974 — Bombed a British military bus in Manchester, England, killing 12.

November 1975 — Murdered Guiness Book of Records editor in London.

July 1976 — Assassinated Christopher Ewart-Briggs, British Ambassador to the Republic of Ireland, with a landmine.

February 1977 — Murdered the British chief of the American-owned DuPont facility in Londonderry.

February 1978 — Killed 12 and wounded 30 in the bombing of a crowded Belfast restaurant.

August 1979 — Assassinated Louis, Earl Mountbatten, member of the Royal Family and respected World War II hero, by setting off a remotely detonated bomb on his yacht. Three others were killed, including his nephew, and three were injured in the blast.

August 1979 — Killed 18 British soldiers and one civilian with a paired bomb attack in Warrenpoint, Northern Ireland.

February 1980 — Killed a British Army colonel in Bielefeld, West Germany.

October 1981 — Detonated a remote-controlled nail bomb outside a British Army barracks in central London; 2 died and 40 were injured.

November 1981 — Claimed the murder of the Rev. Robert Bradford, member of the British Parliament from Belfast.

March 1982 — Shot to death three soldiers and wounded nine bystanders at a police station in Belfast.

July 1982 — Set off two radio-controlled bombs on the same day in two parks in downtown London. In the first attack a bomb left in the trunk of a car exploded while a detachment of the Queen's Household Cavalry was marching by, killing four soldiers. Another bomb exploded under a bandstand, killing seven band members.

The aftermath of an October 1981 PIRA bomb attack at Ebury Bridge Road, near Chelsea Barracks. Two people died in an attack that injured both soldiers and civilians.

December 1983 — Exploded a car bomb outside of Harrods department store, London, killing 5 (including 1 American) and wounding 80.

October 1984 — Narrowly missed killing Prime Minister Margaret Thatcher and her Cabinet with a bomb blast at their Brighton, England, hotel. The bomb blast killed 1 Cabinet member and 3 others and injured 32.

February 1985 — Killed 9 police and wounded 37 others (25 of them civilians) in a mortar attack in Newry.

May 1986 — Killed two Royal Ulster Constabulary (RUC) officers and a British Army major in a landmine attack in County Armagh.

January 1987 — Injured 11 people (including 4 policemen) in a series of bomb attacks in Belfast.

March 1987 — Injured 27 Germans and 4 British subjects in a bomb attack on a British Officers Club in Rheindahlen, West German.

April 1987 — Killed Northern Ireland's second most senior judge and his wife in a car bomb attack on the main road from Dublin to Belfast.

May 1987 — Eight PIRA members were killed in an ambush as they attempted to attack a RUC Station in County Armagh.

May-July 1987 — Eleven police and civilians were killed by ambush in various Northern Ireland locations.

July 1987 — Damaged two hotels in Londonderry, Northern Ireland, with car bombs, but injured no one.

August 1987 — Planted six bombs in a commercial complex outside of Belfast in Dunmurray. Only two detonated, gutting a carpet warehouse and a furniture shop, but causing no injuries because of a PIRA warning.

The PIRA claimed responsibility for this car bomb that exploded outside of Harrods department store in London in December 1983.

October 1987 — Exploded a bomb by the rear entrance of the Royal Courts of Justice in Belfast; no injuries or damage.

November 1987 — Exploded a bomb in Enniskillen in a community center building as numerous people gathered for a war memorial service. Eleven people were killed and 65 injured.

May 1988 — In Roermond, the Netherlands, a gunman fired on three Royal Air Force servicemen leaving a pub, killing one and wounding the other two. Shortly thereafter, a bomb exploded at Nieuw Bergen, killing two of the Royal Air Force airmen in the vehicle in which the bomb was placed.

July 1988 — Exploded a bomb in Duisburg, West Germany, at Glamorgan Army Barracks, tearing off part of the roof and injuring nine members of the Royal Engineer Corps. The bomb was placed near the outside wall of the soldiers' living quarters and caused extensive property damage.

August 1988 — Bombed a Royal Army Engineer postal unit barracks in North London, killing one and injuring nine.

Red Army Faction (RAF)

Date Formed 1968.

Estimated Membership 20-30 hardcore members.

Headquarters Federal Republic of Germany (FRG).

Area of Operations Primarily Federal Republic of Germany.

Leadership Functions with a collective leadership thought to include, among others, Barbara Mayer, Inge Viett, Sigrid Sternbeck, Tomas Simon, Wolfgang Grams, Horst Meyer, Birgit Hogefeld, Silke Maier-Witt, Susanne Albrecht.

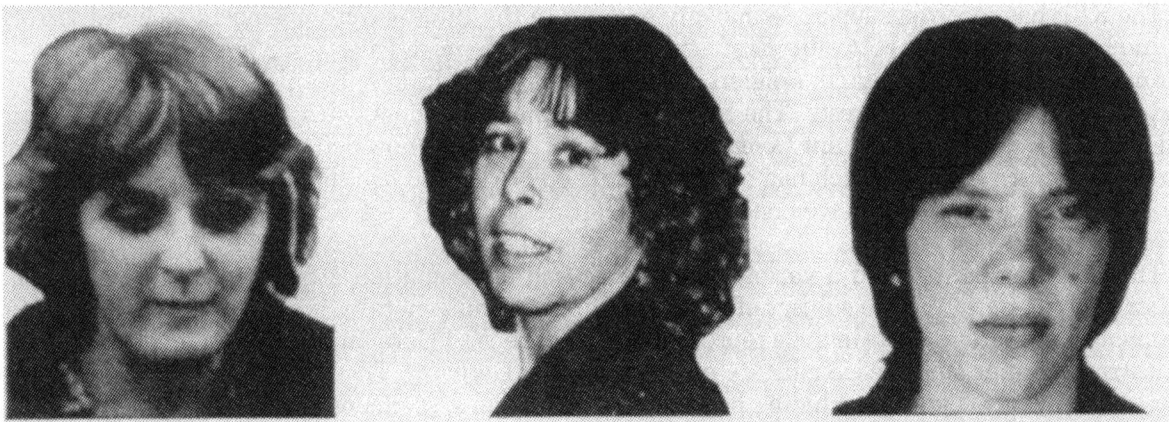

Silke Maier-Witt   Inge Viett   Susanne Albrecht

Members of the leadership of the Red Army Faction.

Other Names Baader Meinhof Gang, Baader Meinhof Group, *Rote Armee Fraktion* (original language).

Sponsors No major foreign sponsors.

Political Objectives/Target Audiences
- Destroy Western capitalism through terrorism, helping precipitate a worldwide Marxist revolution.
- Use terrorism to destroy FRG-US solidarity, especially by attacking American military targets in West Germany.
- Use specific acts of terrorism to try to force authorities to release imprisoned RAF members.

Background

The RAF began as part of the student antiwar movement in the 1960s. Originally called the Baader Meinhof Gang, it was dedicated to general terrorism and antiestablishment activity as part of its perceived role as a stimulus to worldwide Marxist revolution.

The current generation of the RAF hardcore is Marxist-Leninist in ideology. The RAF sees itself as part of an international movement aimed at bringing about a worldwide revolution that would topple existing power structures in the capitalist world.

The RAF has suffered many changes of fortune during its two-decade history. All of its original leaders were captured or forced out of the country by the mid-1970s, but a new and more violent group replaced them. Most of the RAF leadership are well educated. Many have medical, legal, or technical training.

The RAF organizational concept calls for a multilevel structure. The "hardcore" consists of 20-30 combatants who live underground and conduct most of the lethal terrorist activities. West German authorities say the hardcore command level also directs the operations of "illegal militants," who carry out bombings and lower level attacks. The "periphery," of whom there are probably several hundred, form the vital support base that provides necessary funding, shelter, and communications for the operatives. A larger number of legal sympathizers assist in propagandizing RAF ideology.

The RAF has received support from many sectors. In the 1970s, several members received terrorist training at camps in the Middle East, sponsored by extremist Palestinian groups. Contacts are maintained with French, Dutch, Belgian, Danish, Swiss, Irish, Italian, Spanish, and American groups and individuals of like interests. The RAF is one of the cofounders, with the French Direct Action (AD) and the Belgian Combatant Communist Cells (CCC), of the now-defunct Anti-Imperialist Armed Front in Western Europe, which had "declared war" on NATO and had the goal of furthering terrorist cooperation. The RAF may have conducted joint attacks with Direct Action in 1985-86.

The RAF has perpetrated a variety of bombing and assassination attacks over the years. Each major RAF operation is the subject of detailed planning and generally is executed in a professional manner. Major RAF targets include representatives of the West German "establishment," the military-industrial complex, and the US military presence in West Germany. The RAF has access to a large and varied supply of weaponry, including handguns, machineguns, grenades, and RPG-7 rocket-propelled grenades. The RAF also has shown considerable skill in manufacturing improvised explosive devices.

Although the RAF has had an irregular history because of the periodic capture of its primary leaders, the group has shown a disturbing ability to resurface with renewed and vicious attacks. Because of its relatively large support base, it probably will continue to be a serious terrorist threat.

Selected Incident Chronology

May 1972 — Carried out 6 separate bombing attacks, killing 1 and injuring 13, at a US Officers Club in Frankfurt; bombed the vehicle of German Supreme Court Justice Buddenburg, seriously injuring his wife; and killed 3 and wounded 5 in a blast at the US Army European Headquarters in Heidelberg.

November 1974 — Killed German Supreme Court President Guenther von Drenkmann.

February 1975 — Kidnaped two leading German politicians to force the release of six imprisoned terrorists.

April 1977 — Ambushed and murdered German Federal Prosecutor Siegfried Buback, his chauffeur, and a police bodyguard.

September 1977 — Kidnaped German businessman Hanns-Martin Schleyer and killed his chauffeur and three police guards. While the RAF was holding Schleyer, the Popular Front for the Liberation of Palestine hijacked an aircraft in a supporting attack. After German counterterrorist forces successfully foiled the hijacking, the RAF murdered Schleyer.

June 1979 — Attempted assassination of NATO Commander General Alexander Haig, with a bomb concealed under a bridge in Obourg, Belgium. The bomb exploded between General Haig's car and an escort vehicle, wounding two guards.

August 1981 — Bombed the US Air Force headquarters in Ramstein, injuring 18 Americans and 2 Germans.

September 1981 — Fired two RPG-7 grenades at US Army European Commanding General Kroessen's car, slightly injuring his wife and him.

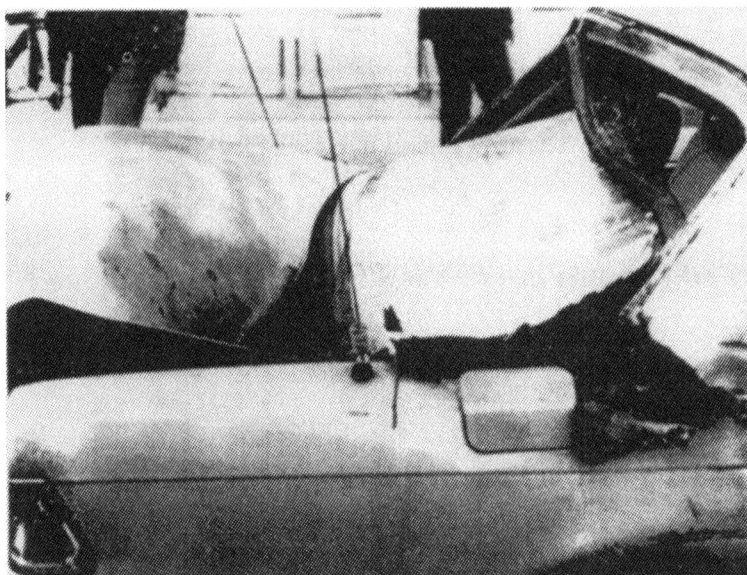

The Mercedes in which US Army European Commanding General Kroessen was riding when Red Army Faction terrorists fired an RPG-7 at the vehicle in September 1981.

December 1984 — Bombed the French Embassy in Bonn and attempted to bomb the NATO School in Oberammergau.

January 1985 — Firebombed the home of the US Consul General in Frankfurt and the US airfield at Heidelberg. Also firebombed a number of West German Government facilities throughout Germany.

February 1985 — Invaded the home of West German businessman Ernst Zimmermann and shot him in the head.

March 1985 — Injured nine with a bomb blast at a department store in Dortmund.

August 1985 — Detonated a car bomb at the Rhein Main Air Base, killing 2 and injuring 17. Terrorists killed an off-duty US serviceman the night before the attack and used his military identification to gain access to the base.

April 1986 — Believed responsible for bombing the NATO fuel pipeline near Vollersode.

May 1986 — Severely damaged a US military fuel pumping station and destroyed two trucks with a bomb that also ignited over 1,000 gallons of fuel.

July 1986 — Killed Karl-Heinz Beckurts, Director of Research of the Siemens Electronics Company, and his chauffeur with a remotely detonated bomb. The RAF claimed it was because of Beckurts' advocacy of nuclear energy and research participation in the Strategic Defense Initiative project.

October 1986 — Murdered Gerold von Braunmuehl, head of the Foreign Ministry's political department. He was shot in front of his home in Bonn.

Red Brigades (BR)

Date Formed 1970.

Estimated Membership Approximately 50-75 hardcore terrorists.

Headquarters Rome, Naples, Genoa, Milan, and the Tuscany region of central Italy.

Area of Operations Italy.

Leadership Most prominent BR leaders are currently in jail. The identities of current leaders at large are not known.

Other Names *Brigate Rosse* (original language).

Sponsors None known.

Political Objectives/Target Audiences
- Destroy the Government of Italy through revolutionary action.
- Oppose the presence of NATO by creating fear among NATO personnel stationed in Italy.
- Carry out a campaign of destruction directed at "imperialist multinational corporations."

Background

The Red Brigades has been one of the most lethal of the major European terrorist groups. It has conducted an extensive number of attacks with murder, "kneecaping," and kidnaping as its favored terrorist tactics. Preferred targets have been representatives of the Italian "establishment" whom it considers the "oppressors of society." These individuals include business executives, members of the police judiciary and legal professions, and political party activists. Attacks have been characterized by precise planning and execution.

The BR was spawned by the ultraradical wing of the Italian labor movement. Although the BR began with a clear focus on destroying the Italian establishment, it expanded its horizons in late 1981 when it "declared war" on NATO, and in early 1984 when it expressed solidarity with Middle Eastern terrorist groups. Recently the group's propaganda has offered support to the idea of increasing contacts and cooperation among West European terrorist groups and of targeting individuals and institutions involved in Strategic Defense Initiative research.

The BR organizational structure is believed to be highly cellular and strictly compartmentalized, helping to ensure security and independent action by the various units. In the late 1970s and early

1980s, the Italian police succeeded in arresting many BR leaders and confiscating large amounts of arms and explosives. In 1987, with the cooperation of French and Spanish authorities, the Italians succeeded in apprehending numerous BR terrorists, including those responsible for the March 1987 assassination of Italian Air Force General Lucio Giorgieri. While drastically reducing the operational capability of the BR, police action has not totally destroyed the organization.

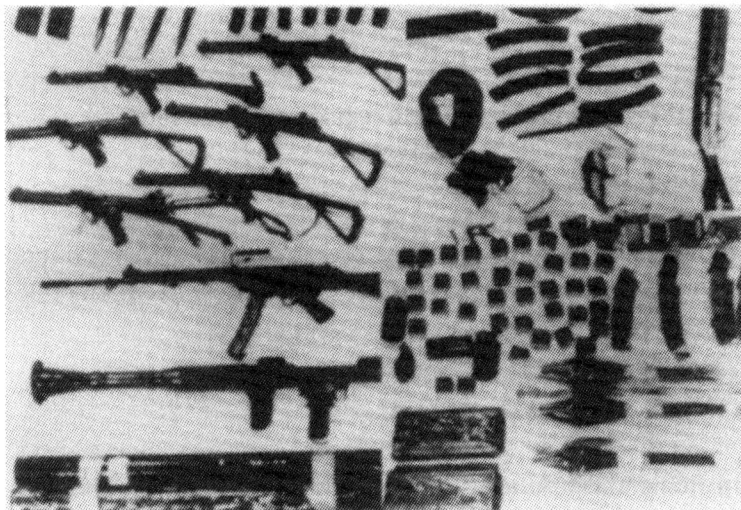

A Red Brigades arms cache found by Italian police in a wooded area near Treviso in February 1982 included such items as an RPG-7.

Two separate factions appear to have developed within the BR since 1984. One faction, the Militarists or the Fighting Communist Party (PCC), constitutes the majority and usually follows a strict Leninist view that only violent terrorist acts can pave the way for revolution. The other faction, the Movementalists or Union of Fighting Communists (UCC), is the minority or splinter group that does not believe a revolution is possible until the proletariat has been sufficiently politicized to support revolutionary action. Regardless of differences in rhetoric, the two groups show little difference in either method of operation or targeting.

The BR has had contacts with the West German Red Army Faction (RAF) and the French Direct Action (AD) organization. BR members have been arrested in France in the company of AD militants. Large numbers of BR militants enjoy safehaven in France, and evidence points to the existence of a BR "external column" whose task is to "protect fugitives and recruit new militants." Recent arrests also indicate a BR presence in Spain.

The BR also may have ties to Palestinian terrorist groups. In the late 1970s, BR members smuggled into Italy at least two shipments of weapons provided by Palestinian elements. Training of BR militants in Palestinian camps in Lebanon also has been alleged. Moreover, the BR is suspected of involvement, along with the Lebanese Armed Revolutionary Faction, in the 1984 assassination of American Leamon Hunt, Director General of the Multinational Force and Observers for the Sinai.

Selected Incident Chronology

April 1974 — Kidnaped Public Prosecutor Mario Rossi and killed his two bodyguards. Rossi was held in a "people's prison" for 35 days, then released.

June 1976 — Killed Chief Prosecutor Francesco Coco and his two police guards in Genoa.

April 1977 — Murdered attorney Fulvio Croce, President of the Turin Bar Association.

March 1978 — Kidnaped Christian Democratic Party President Aldo Moro and killed his chauffeur, his bodyguard, and three police in the abduction. Moro was held for 2 months before being murdered.

May 1979 — Set off bombs in the Christian Democratic Party building in Rome, killing two and injuring one.

January 1980 — Claimed the murder of the President of the Sicilian regional government.

May 1980 — Killed a senior police official in Mestre.

April 1981 — Killed two guards and wounded a secretary while kidnaping Naples City Councilor Ciro Cirillo. He was held until July, when he was released through "revolutionary magnanimity" and the payment of a $1.2 million ransom.

December 1981 — Kidnaped US Army Brigadier General James Dozier in Verona. He was held for 42 days until freed in a rescue operation by Italian counterterrorist forces.

April 1982 — Ambushed a police van in Rome and wounded three policemen in the machinegun and grenade attack.

October 1982 — During a bank robbery in Turin, killed two unarmed bank guards.

January 1983 — Murdered a female prison guard in Rome after subjecting her to a "people's trial."

February 1984 — Claimed responsibility for the assassination of US citizen Leamon Hunt, Director General, Multinational Force and Observers (responsible for monitoring the peace accord between Egypt and Israel). Operation may have been in conjunction with the Lebanese Armed Revolutionary Faction.

March 1985 — Murdered Enzio Tarantelli, a University of Rome economics professor and labor union official.

February 1986 — Shot and killed former Florence Mayor Lando Conti.

February 1986 — Attempted to murder Antonio da Empoli, economic adviser to Prime Minister Bettino Craxi. Da Empoli was slightly wounded. His bodyguard killed one terrorist and wounded a second, both female; a male assailant escaped on a motorcycle.

February 1987 — Attacked a postal van and a police escort vehicle in Rome. Killed two policemen and wounded a third. Escaped with over $800,000 from the van.

March 1987 — Shot and killed Air Force General Lucio Giorgieri, Director General of Italian Space and Air Armaments. The two gunmen on a motorcycle escaped in Rome traffic.

Revolutionary Cells (RZ)

Date Formed 1973.

Estimated Membership 100.

Headquarters West Berlin and Frankfurt am Main.

Area of Operations West Germany.

Leadership Rudolph Raabe, Sonja Suder, Christian Gauger, Rudolf Schindler, Sabine Eckle.

Other Names *Revolutionaere Zellen, Rote Zora* (original language).

Sponsors No known foreign sponsors.

Political Objectives/Target Audiences
- Conduct "urban guerrilla" terrorist activity in support of "antifascism," "anti-imperialism," "anti-Zionism," and "antimilitarism."
- Pressure US forces in West Germany through terrorist attacks that create fear and suspicion.
- Destroy the West German "system" with terrorism.

Background

The Revolutionary Cells sums up its organizational goals with these words: "We will not hesitate from shooting, bombing, extortion, and taking hostages. The whole ruling class will be made to feel insecure." The RZ put these words into action in October 1986 when two gunmen shot and wounded a West German Government official. The last shooting incident attributed to the RZ prior to this attack had been the "accidental" assassination of the Economics Minister of Hesse in 1981.

The RZ occasionally has been linked with the Red Army Faction, but normally tries to keep its distance. The RZ believes in a decentralized form of terrorism directed at targets within the immediate vicinity of each cell. To achieve maximum security, its cells typically are composed of less than 10 members with minimal contact between cells.

The RZ is believed to have picked up members from small, defunct antiestablishment radical groups of the early 1970s. In addition, one former terrorist and police informer claimed that the RZ has ties to Palestinian terrorist organizations. Ties to other European Marxist or anarchist groups undoubtedly exist. The RZ is believed to have contacts with the Irish National Liberation Army and the Provisional Irish Republican Army.

In its publication *Revolutionaere Zorn* ("Revolutionary Wrath"), the RZ declared its intent to "immediately and everywhere begin the armed struggle." In the same publication, it further contends that the situation is a "struggle of workers, youth, and women." Within the RZ is an autonomous womens' group, *Rote Zora*, that professes a doctrine of struggle against exploitation of the Third World, repression of women, sexism, and racism.

The RZ wants a pool of semi-independent strike teams to be spread across Germany and carefully "covered" by the appearance of normal civilian lifestyles. From this position, they can strike quickly and without warning at a variety of locations and without the need to set up elaborate chains of support.

RZ members have given evidence of mastery of a wide variety of terrorist skills. They not only are competent with standard military weapons, but also can make their own explosives and sophisticated timing devices. Their favorite method of attack is the time-delayed bomb. West German authorities report that the RZ has significant caches of weapons in rural forest areas.

The RZ has targeted US military facilities in West Germany to oppose America's "neocolonialist" military presence in the FRG.

In 1986-87, the RZ embarked upon a terror campaign protesting West Germany's "anti-immigration" policies.

Selected Incident Chronology

June 1976 — Bombed the US Army V Corps Headquarters in Frankfurt, injuring 16.

December 1976 — Bombed the US Air Force Officers Club at Rhein Main Air Base, injuring seven.

May 1977 — Attempted to kidnap the Roman Catholic Archbishop of Cologne, to exchange for imprisoned terrorists. Police foiled the attempt.

May 1978 — Shot and wounded a court-appointed terrorist defense attorney and set a car bomb in the auto of another (the bomb was defused before it detonated).

December 1979 — Bombed the Frankfurt office of the Morgan Trust Company of New York, causing property damage.

November 1980 — Firebombed the Munich office of the West German Draft Board.

May 1981 — Claimed responsibility for the murder of the West German Economics Minister of Hesse, Heinz Karry. In a message the RZ said: "The death of Karry was not intended, but (rather) an accident. The plan was to keep him in bed for a long time by shooting him in the legs."

October 1981 — Bombed the offices of a Frankfurt construction company.

June 1982 — Detonated a bomb on a bicycle outside a US Army communications center in Frankfurt.

January-November 1983 — Carried out 19 bombings and incendiary attacks on Government facilities and civilian companies.

May 1983 — Bombed the US Officers Club in Bamberg.

February 1984 — Claimed responsibility for bombing the Turkish Consulate in Cologne.

June 1984 — Bombed the NATO fuel pipeline near Lorch in Baden-Wurttemberg.

December 1984 — Bombed a US military office building in Duesseldorf.

March 1985 — Claimed responsibility for bombings at mining and shipping offices in Bochum, Essen, and Hamburg.

January-October 1986 — Carried out bombings and incendiary attacks in several cities, some on the same day, targeting private businesses and public institutions.

October 1986 — Shot and wounded the chief of the West Berlin Foreigners' Registry Office. Claimed responsibility for bombing a Lufthansa office in Cologne on the same day.

February 1987 — Bombed the Central Welfare Office for Asylum Seekers in West Berlin.

March 1987 — Bombed the Alien Welfare Office in West Berlin.

April 1987 — Set off incendiary devices, causing damage to Government offices in Augsburg.

June 1987 — Committed arson attack on a chemical plant (Rhine-Westphalian Electric Power Company) at Kelsterbach, causing several hundred thousand dollars' damage.

August 1987 — Attempted to bomb a US military train, but because of a schedule change, a freight train detonated the bomb, near Hedemlenden.

August 1987 — Committed arson attacks at nine branches of the German clothing firm Adler.

November 1987 — Conducted incendiary attack in the parking lot of a vehicle depot owned by a grocery chain, completely destroying 15 trucks; no injuries.

Revolutionary Organization 17 November

Date Formed 1975.

Estimated Membership Approximately 20-25.

Headquarters Believed to be in Athens.

Area of Operations Athens.

Leadership Unknown.

Other Names *Epanastaiki Organosi 17 Noemvri* (original language).

Sponsors None known.

Political Objectives/Target Audiences
- Force Greece out of NATO and end the US military presence in Greece.
- Oppose imperialism and capitialism.

Background

Since its first appearance in December 1975, when it claimed responsibility for assassination of US Embassy officer Richard Welch in Athens, the 17 November has established itself as one of the most proficient and lethal terrorist groups in Europe. Marxist in orientation and virulently anti-US, the group has conducted attacks against Greek targets it considers to oppose the revolution and official US personnel who represent "interference" in Greek affairs.

The 17 November attacks have been almost exclusively ambush-style assassinations by two- to three-member teams. Victims usually are attacked near their homes or offices. A unique 17 November characteristic has been to use the same pistol in several of its attacks, including the assassinations of two Americans. This could indicate that the group has limited resources, or it may be its method to "authenticate" its responsibility for attacks. In any case, using the same pistol indicates that the group is confident of its ability to elude the police. In fact, not a single 17 November member has been arrested in nearly 13 years of attacks. The 17 November organization has been responsible for several bombings since 1985, including an attack against a bus transporting US military personnel in April 1987 that injured 18. The 17 November organization also claimed responsibility for an August 1987 bomb attack against another bus carrying US military personnel; 12 were injured, 10 of them Americans. Within the last 12 months, the frequency of 17 November attacks has increased considerably, while the use of bombs to cause indiscriminate injuries gives the 17 November additional capability and poses an added threat.

Little is known concerning the 17 November's membership, organization, or relationships, if any, to other Greek terrorist groups. Following an October 1987 shootout between police and members of the Revolutionary Popular Struggle (ELA), however, and a subsequent search of ELA hideouts, Greek police believe they established a link between the two groups. There is no evidence that the 17 November maintains ties to foreign terrorist groups.

Selected Incident Chronology

December 1975 — Assassinated US Embassy officer Richard Welch.

January 1979 — Killed a Greek police officer.

January 1980 — Killed the deputy chief of the Greek Riot Police and his chauffeur.

November 1983 — Assassinated US Navy Captain George Tsantes and his driver.

April 1984 — Shot and wounded US Army Master Sergeant Robert Judd as he was transporting documents. Master Sergeant Judd probably saved his life by being alert and taking evasive action when he noticed the two terrorists approach his car on a motorcycle.

February 1985 — Assassinated conservative Greek newspaper editor Nikos Momferatos and his chauffeur. The communique claiming responsibility denounced the journalist as one of the "fascist agents of the CIA."

November 1985 — Claimed responsibility for bombing a Greek police bus, killing one policeman.

April 1986 — Killed retired Greek industrialist Dimitrios Angelopoulos.

Diagram of the assassination attack in Greece against Captain Tsantes.

In November 1983, the Revolutionary Organization 17 November attacked this automobile, in which US Navy Captain Tsantes was riding. He and his driver were killed.

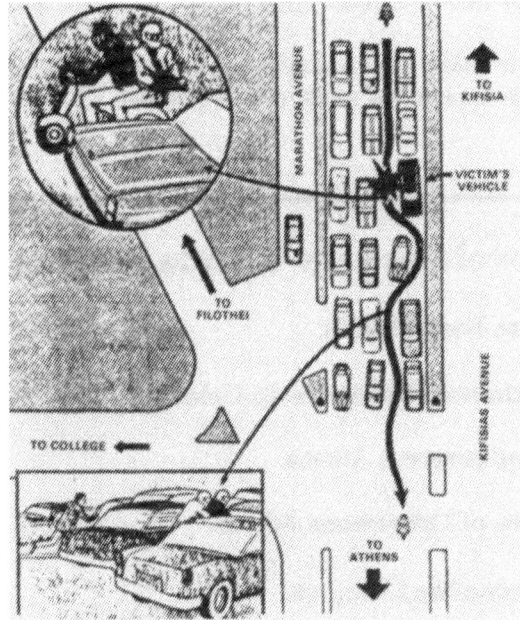

October 1986 — Claimed responsibility for bombing four Greek Government offices, including three tax offices. The 17 November communique denounced the current Greek tax system. (The ELA also claimed responsibility for the bombings.)

February 1987 — Claimed responsibility for maiming Zakharias Kapsalakis, a wealthy Greek physician.

April 1987 — Bombed a bus carrying US and Greek military personnel near Athens, injuring 18, including 16 Americans.

August 1987 — Bombed a US bus in Voula, injuring 10 US servicemen.

January 1988 — Attempted assassination of a DEA agent in Athens.

A bomb explosion destroyed a crowded bar filled with US soldiers in Athens, Greece. Twenty-seven Americans were injured in the February 1985 attack.

Members of the US military forces in Greece view the wreckage of a US car destroyed by a bomb. Three cars were gutted and two damaged in the July 1985 attack in Athens.

Neither incident has been attributed to a known terrorist group.

May 1988 — Placed high-explosive bombs on two automobiles belonging to the Turkish Embassy.

June 1988 — Detonated a car bomb that killed US Defense Attache Captian William Nordeen shortly after he left his residence in Athens.

Revolutionary Popular Struggle (ELA)

Date Formed 1973.

Estimated Membership Unknown.

Headquarters Athens.

Area of Operations Athens.

Leadership Unknown.

Other Names *Epanastikos Laikos Agonas* (original language).

Sponsors None known.

Political Objectives/Target Audiences
- Force Greece out of NATO and eliminate the US military presence in Greece.
- Strike against "fascism and imperialism" as a stimulus to revolution.

Background

The ELA is an extreme leftist group that developed out of the opposition to the military junta that ruled Greece from 1967 to 1974. It has declared its opposition to "imperialist domination, exploitation, and oppression." The ELA is strongly anti-US and seeks the removal of US military forces from Greece. To support its goals, the group has carried out a series of relatively unsophisticated bombings against Greek Government and economic targets as well as US interests. To date ELA-claimed incidents have caused only property damage and no injuries.

Little is known about the ELA's structure, membership, and relationships, if any, to other Greek terrorist groups. There has been speculation that the ELA in some way provides support or coordination to other terrorist organizations in Greece. Analysis of the ELA is further complicated by the periodic appearance of several, apparently new, groups claiming responsibility for acts of terrorism in Greece. It is possible that these names are nothing more than covers used by the ELA or another group to confuse authorities and to project a growing revolutionary movement. Although details concerning the relationships between Greek terrorist groups are sketchy, Greek police believe they have established a link between the ELA and the 17 November organization.

Although the ELA has expressed solidarity with other terrorist groups and revolutionary movements, including the West German Red Army Faction and the French Direct Action, there is no evidence that the group maintains ties to foreign terrorist groups.

Selected Incident Chronology

November 1975 — Firebombed the US Air Force commissary in Athens.

October 1977 — Detonated a bomb outside the US Air Force Noncommissioned Officers Club in Glyfada.

January 1978 — Bombed the US Information Agency and American Express offices in Athens to protest a visit by US Secretary of State Cyrus Vance.

May 1980 — Claimed responsibility for firebombing 17 Greek- and foreign-owned vehicles in the Athens area.

May 1981 — Bombed an unoccupied vehicle owned by an employee of the US Embassy.

April 1982 — Firebombed the unoccupied car of a US Embassy employee.

June 1982 — Detonated four bombs in Athens to protest the visit of US General Bernard Rogers, Supreme Allied Commander Europe.

March 1986 — Bombed the Hellenic-American Union in Athens to protest the visit of US Secretary of State George Shultz.

September 1987 — Bombed the US Air Force commissary in Athens.

October 1987 — Conducted a shootout with Greek police; two suspected terrorists apprehended, one fatally wounded.

May 1988 — Conducted three bombings in Piraeus, Greece, against a police station, a discotheque, and a pub, causing substantial damage but no injuries.

Latin American Terrorism

Terrorist attacks against official or high-visibility US targets in Latin America have occurred intermittently since the rise of Fidel Castro in Cuba. Since 1979, however, Latin American terrorism generally has been on the rise, attributable largely to the inspiration provided by the success of the Sandinista movement in Nicaragua, as well as renewed Cuban enthusiasm for promoting revolutionary violence.

Terrorism in Latin America is frequently an indicator of the initial phase of a fledgling insurgent movement that has as its eventual goal the development of full-scale guerrilla warfare. Terrorist tactics also are likely to be used as a kind of fallback to demonstrate that the group continues to be a viable threat, even though its insurgent forces may be experiencing setbacks. In addition, the illegal narcotics trade has increased the sporadic interaction between narcotics traffickers and these groups in recent years.

Latin American terrorism differs from that in Western Europe and the Middle East because transnational terrorism to date has not become a significant element in the threat to US citizens in the region. Latin American groups tend to be highly nationalistic, even though they frequently benefit from external support such as military training, funding, and material, especially from Cuba and Nicaragua. Neither transnational coordination nor foreign direction of operational planning has been characteristic.

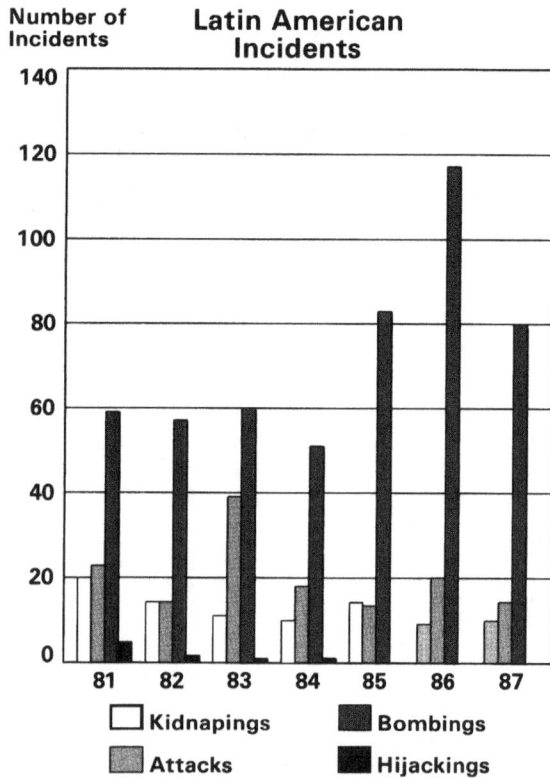

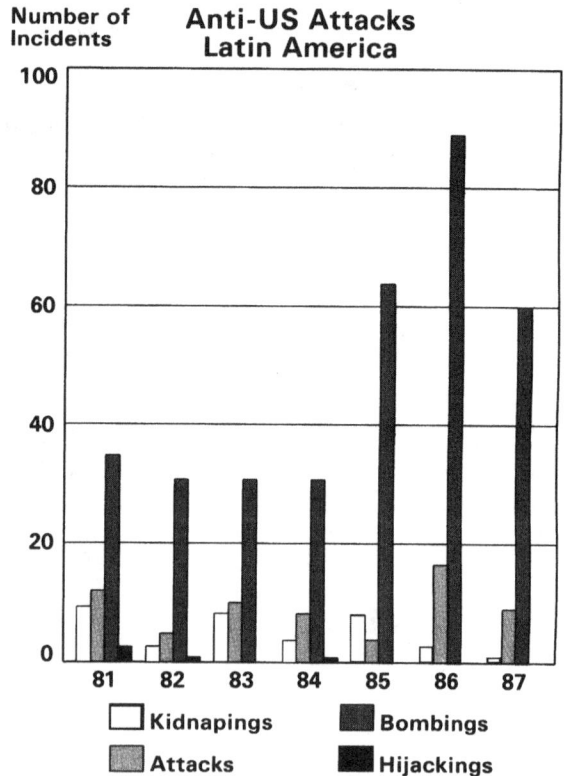

Number of Incidents

Latin American Incidents

Kidnapings — Bombings
Attacks — Hijackings

Number of Incidents

Anti-US Attacks Latin America

Kidnapings — Bombings
Attacks — Hijackings

Increased efforts against international narcotics trafficking are generating growing violent reactions from the narcotics traffickers, who often employ the tactics of terror. A marriage of convenience between some traffickers and insurgents occasionally has produced common objectives, as in Colombia, where assassination-for-hire arrangements have occurred between narcotics dealers and leftist terrorists.

Most acts of anti-US terrorism in Latin America have been directed against official US facilities and other symbols of US presence and influence. The most frequent targets have been embassies, ambassadors' residences, or less secure facilities such as binational or bicultural centers and US businesses. The most common methods of attack have been dynamite bombings and strafing with automatic weapons fire. Though not usually targeted, US citizens have been involved in at least 18 significant attacks since 1979. Most of these have occurred in Colombia, Honduras, and El Salvador and to a lesser extent, Guatemala, Costa Rica, and Peru.

In Chile, the Manuel Rodriguez Patriotic Front has become increasingly bold. Although this organization's targeting is directed primarily against the Pinochet regime, US facilities also have been attacked.

In the French departments of Guadaloupe, Martinique, and French Guyana, Libya has made efforts to gain influence with radical groups, with the shared objective of undermining French authority there.

Alfaro Lives, Damn It! (AVC)

Date Formed 1983.

Estimated Membership 200-300.

Headquarters Unknown.

Area of Operations Ecuador, particularly urban areas such as Quito and Guayaquil.

Leadership Currently in question because of arrests or deaths of most of its senior leaders in 1986 and 1987.

Other Names *Alfaro Vive, Carajo!* (original language).

Sponsors M-19 of Colombia, and probably Cuba, Libya, and Nicaragua.

Political Objectives/Target Audiences
- Little is known about the political agenda of the AVC, except that the group favors social "reform" and opposes "oligarchy and imperialism."
- Create opposition to the current Government, especially among the rural poor.
- Force the withdrawal of US and other foreign interests from Ecuador.

Background

The AVC initiated armed activities in August 1983 — in the same fashion used earlier by the Colombian M-19 — by stealing swords used by an Ecuadorean national hero, Eloy Alfaro, a revolutionary leader and President of Ecuador in the early 20th century, who was killed in 1912.

Through early 1986, the AVC carried out a number of bank robberies, kidnapings, and minor bombings.

The AVC claims to be non-Marxist, but at least some of its members are known to have ties to Cuba and Nicaragua. When AVC leader Rosa Cardenas was arrested in September 1984, she was carrying documents that confirmed these ties and suggested plans to approach Libya.

Documents confiscated at the AVC headquarters, raided in March 1986, provided evidence of Libyan involvement in the training of AVC members. The evidence included the passenger lists of Iberian Airlines flights from Quito to Madrid, which showed 20 Ecuadoreans whose reservations included connecting flights to Tripoli. One of that group was arrested during the March 1986 raid.

The AVC has sent personnel to Colombia for training and participation in military operations, under the leadership of the M-19, in the multinational unit known as the America Battalion. By June 1986, the M-19 reportedly had trained some 40 AVC rebels. The AVC reportedly also collaborated with Peru's Tupac Amaru Revolutionary Movement (MRTA), possibly through MRTA participation in the America Battalion.

Many of the AVC's terrorist acts have been in search of publicity. The group tries to use the public news media and its own pamphlets to spread its message.

Financing for AVC operations evidently comes primarily from bank robberies. AVC members hope for Libyan or Cuban financial support, and many receive a small amount.

Throughout 1986 and 1987, the AVC suffered serious setbacks from Government security forces. Essentially leaderless and disorganized, the group has conducted little terrorist activity since mid-1986.

Selected Incident Chronology

August 1983 — Raided the Guayaquil Museum and stole swords that belonged to Eloy Alfaro.

May 1984 — Exploded a large bomb in the back of the US Embassy compound in Quito.

October 1984 — Briefly occupied the Costa Rican Embassy to protest that nation's extradition of AVC leader Rosa Cardenas.

September 1985 — Kidnaped a prominent Ecuadoran banker, who was later killed in a rescue attempt.

October 1985 — Occupied the Mexican Embassy and used its telex system to send a message to Latin American nations protesting the break in diplomatic relations between Ecuador and Nicaragua, and denouncing US support for the Nicaraguan contras.

February 1986 — Seized a radio station and broadcast a propaganda tape celebrating the group's third anniversary.

May 1986 — Kidnaped a member of the Constitutional Court, who was freed after a negotiated surrender.

April 1987 — Bombed a police station in Quito, damaging 20 vehicles.

Bandera Roja (Red Flag — GBR)

Date Formed 1969.

Estimated Membership Less than 50 in the armed wing.

Headquarters Unknown.

Area of Operations Eastern Venezuela and along Venezuela-Colombia border.

Leadership Current leadership is in question since Gabriel *Puerta* Aponte was imprisoned in 1982, former leader Carlos Betancourt was imprisoned in 1977, and Julio Escalona accepted a Presidential pardon in May 1979.

Other Names *Frente Americo Silva* (Americo Silva Front — FAS) is the GBR's armed wing (original language).

Sponsors Cuba is reported to have abandoned support for guerrilla warfare in Venezuela in 1969.

Political Objectives/Target Audiences
- Began originally as a Marxist-Leninist program of rural revolution, but rejected the Venezuelan constitutional left, including the Venezuelan Communist Party and the Movement of the Revolutionary Left.
- Political agenda later called for establishing a "dictatorship of the proletariat in Venezuela by means of an armed struggle."
- Shun the leftist elements that have accepted legal status and are seeking elections as a means of obtaining power.

Background

The Red Flag splintered from the Venezuelan Movement of the Revolutionary Left (MIR) in 1969, when the Soviet Union decided to pursue diplomatic relations with Venezuela and force Cuba to abandon support for insurgents in Venezuela. The group was led through the early 1970s by Carlos Betancourt and Gabriel *Puerta* Aponte.

In 1972, in a joint operation with the MIR, the Red Flag kidnaped Carlos Dominguez Chavez, a Caracas industrialist, and received $1 million in ransom. Betancourt and Puerta were captured in 1973, but escaped from Caracas' top-security prison in 1975.

In that same year, the Red Flag rejected the constitutional left. It also issued a death list condemning 20 men prominent in agriculture and began abduction of wealthy businessmen for ransom.

Sporadic Red Flag operations, such as ambushes of military vehicles and temporary takeovers of small towns, occurred in 1976 and 1977. Betancourt was recaptured in 1977, and Red Flag activity all but stopped by 1979.

The Red Flag resurfaced in December 1981 with the hijacking of three domestic flights, demanding a ransom and the release of prisoners. The group did not intimidate the Venezuelan Government, which captured Puerta in April 1982 and killed 25 militants in an ensuing firefight.

The group apparently has been unable to secure any outside sponsorship and probably relies on ransoms from kidnaping and hijacking, as well as raids on small towns. To support itself the Red Flag apparently has some contact with two Colombian revolutionary groups, the National Liberation Army and 19th of April Movement.

With the decline in the oil market and the subsequent effect on the Venezuelan economy, there is a possibility that the Red Flag could find renewed support among the economically distressed. The terrorists face many obstacles, though, such as their lack of external support, the loyalty and effectiveness of the Venezuelan security forces, and offers of political amnesty for guerrillas. With its guerrilla front dormant, most of the GBR's present activity appears to be limited to political activism on university campuses and attempts to gain influence with labor unions.

Selected Incident Chronology

April 1979 — Raided the Maracay branch of the National Directory for Identification and Foreign Documentation, Aragua State; stole 27,000 validated civilian identification documents, 40,000 blank civilian identification documents, 300 blank passports, official seals, 6 typewriters, and a document processing machine.

September 1980 — Suspected of robbing a securities firm in Valencia (200 kilometers west of Caracas) of nearly $2 million and 50 light weapons.

November 1981 — Occupied the town of Santa Maria de Ipiere in the eastern state of Guarico. The 30 terrorists attacked the National Guard post, killed a soldier, and stole a number of arms. One terrorist was killed and several others wounded. (No actions have been definitely attributed to the Red Flag since 1981).

September 1984 — The Government feared that the Red Flag and other cells were regrouping after a meeting held with Colombian guerrillas in the state of Guarico.

Cinchoneros Popular Liberation Movement (MPL)

Date Formed 1980.

Estimated Membership Under 200.

Headquarters Tegucigalpa, Honduras (although much of the leadership is in exile).

Areas of Operation Honduras, primarily urban-based, operating out of Tegucigalpa and San Pedro Sula.

Leadership Unknown.

Other Names *Movimiento Popular de Liberacion* (original language).

The primary operating areas of the urban-based Cinchoneros Popular Liberation Movement are Tegucigalpa and San Pedro Sula.

Sponsors Some Cuban and Nicaraguan support; also some sporadic involvement with the Salvadoran Farabundo Marti National Liberation Front.

Political Objectives/Target Audiences

- Espouse a Marxist-Leninist, anti-US dogma. Publicly style itself as an anti-imperialist, antioligarchic, popular, and democratic group.
- Seek to overthrow the Government of Honduras, which defends alleged US "imperialist monopolies."
- The Nicaraguan Sandinistas use their close contact with the MPL to apply leverage against the Government of Honduras and to counter US policy initiatives in the region.

Background

The Cinchoneros Popular Liberation Movement (MPL) is the armed wing of the People's Revolutionary Union (URP), which is one of many splinter groups of the Honduran Communist Party. The Cinchoneros formed in 1980 at the same time the URP appeared and takes its name from the Honduran peasant leader Serapio "Cinchonero" Romero, who was executed in 1865 for refusing to pay tax to the Roman Catholic Church.

The group was one of the two most active Honduran terrorist organizations in the early 1980s, the other being the Lorenzo Zelaya Popular Revolutionary Forces.

Cinchonero terrorist activities have consisted mostly of bombings in San Pedro Sula and Tegucigalpa, and one hostage-taking incident. Honduran security forces arrested several key Cinchonero personalities in the first 7 months of 1984. One arrest uncovered several weapons, blocks of TNT, detonators, and subversive literature.

The MPL apparently funds itself mainly by kidnaping businessmen and robbing banks. Cuba also may provide money as well as training, arms, logistics, and political support.

The Cinchoneros' other significant foreign ties appear to be with Salvadoran guerrilla groups. Salvadoran Farabundo Marti National Liberation Front members reportedly have provided some training and carried out joint kidnapings with the Cinchoneros inside Honduras. The Cinchoneros also are linked to the Sandinista government in Nicaragua and probably receive on-the-job training in jungle warfare against the rebels in Nicaragua. In addition to arms and money, Managua also may be furnishing safehaven, logistical, and political support.

The group currently appears to be rebuilding and has exploded some "propaganda" bombs in the capital to revive public awareness of its existence.

Selected Incident Chronology

April 1980 — Kidnaped the vice president of Texaco, a Costa Rican-born US citizen, in downtown San Pedro Sula. The operation was aborted after Government security forces arrested several participants, and the victim subsequently escaped.

August 1980 — Occupied the offices of the Organization of American States in Tegucigalpa and held several hostages for 2 days. The incident was later resolved peacefully.

March 1981 — Hijacked a New Orleans-bound Honduran Air Services jetliner shortly after takeoff from Tegucigalpa. The 4 armed hijackers later surrendered in exchange for the release of 13 Salvadoran activists from Honduran jails.

September 1982 — Took approximately 100 hostages in a raid on an economics conference in San Pedro Sula. A watchman was killed and two businessmen were wounded during the takeover. The terrorists demanded the release of nine alleged political prisoners. They later surrendered and were permitted to leave for Cuba.

August 1983 — Exploded three time bombs, two at installations belonging to US corporations in San Pedro Sula.

September 1983 — Exploded a bomb in San Pedro Sula at the offices of Costa Rican, Honduran, and US airlines in retaliation for a bombing raid in Nicaragua by an anti-Sandinista guerrilla group.

March 1984 — Exploded five bombs in 1 day in two major cities, Tegucigalpa and San Pedro Sula. A guard reportedly was killed at one location.

October 1987 — Briefly took over two radio stations in San Pedro Sula and one in El Progreso, forcing stations to broadcast Cinchonero propaganda.

Clara Elizabeth Ramirez Front (CERF)

Date Formed 1983.

Estimated Membership 10-20.

Headquarters San Salvador.

Area of Operations San Salvador.

Leadership Unknown.

Other Names *Frente Clara Elizabeth Ramirez* (original language). Sometimes refers to itself by the name of its parent organization, the Popular Liberation Forces (FPL), even though the FPL has ostracized the CERF.

Sponsors No external sponsors known.

Political Objectives/Target Audiences
- Conduct high-visibility acts of urban terrorism to undercut Government efforts to end political violence and erode public support for the Government.
- Target US citizens in El Salvador involved in supporting the Salvadoran Government.

Background

The CERF is a splinter element of the Popular Liberation Forces (FPL). It is led by renegade members of the FPL's urban infrastructure and takes its name from the FPL designation for its metropolitan San Salvador front. Because of its preference for high-visibility and politically inflammatory terrorist attacks, the CERF is considered one of the most radical elements in the Salvadoran insurgency movement. The controversial and unauthorized nature of its attacks have drawn denunciations and rejection from the FPL and other members of the Farabundo Marti National Liberation Front (FMLN). Consequently, CERF actions are probably outside the control of the FMLN.

Little is known about the organizational structure of the CERF except that it is very small and extremely security conscious. The CERF specializes in assassination and operates in an urban setting, unlike many of the other Salvadoran leftist radical groups that conduct primarily rural guerrilla operations. CERF members are believed to be highly trained and quite skillful. Some may have been trained at Cuban bases as part of Cuban support to the FPL before CERF relations with its parent group were severed.

The CERF has shown high interest in US targets, and it remains a potential threat to US military personnel in El Salvador. Intensive and successful counterterrorist operations directed against the CERF by the Salvadoran Government in mid-1985, however, apparently degraded its operational capability, and it has not been active since that time. The threat from the CERF has thus been diluted considerably.

Nevertheless, renewed operations are possible because of the militancy of its members. Current CERF activity appears concentrated on recruitment and political organizing efforts on university campuses and in labor unions.

Selected Incident Chronology

May 1983 — Shot and killed US Navy Lieutenant Commander Albert Schaufelberger as he sat in his auto. (Responsibility for this act was claimed in the name of the FPL.)

November 1984 — Assassinated a Salvadoran guard of the US Embassy a few blocks from the embassy.

November 1984 — Attacked the US Embassy with small arms fire.

December 1984 — Machinegunned the Honduran Embassy building as a protest against the presence of US forces in Honduras.

March 1985 — Shot and killed LTC Ricardo Cienfuegos, top military spokesman for the Salvadoran Armed Forces, at a downtown athletic club. The assassination was conducted without attracting attention, and the killers left their flag draped over Cienfuegos' head when they left.

March 1985 — Shot and killed retired Salvadoran Army General Jose Alberto Medrano, founder of the paramilitary organization ORDEN.

Early 1987 — CERF student front groups in the forefront of increasingly aggressive and militant demonstrations at the US Embassy in San Salvador.

Farabundo Marti National Liberation Front (FMLN)

Date Formed 1980.

Estimated Membership 7,500.

Headquarters Various locations inside El Salvador, with other key offices in Managua, Nicaragua.

Area of Operations El Salvador; some limited operations inside Honduras.

Leadership Joaquin Villalobos (AKA Rene Cruz), Jorge Shafick Handal (AKA Simon), Leonel Gonzalez (AKA Salvador Sanchez), Eduardo Sancho Castaneda (AKA Ferman Cienfuegos), and Francisco Jovel (AKA Roberto Roca) — one each from the five component groups.

Other Names *Frente Farabundo Marti de Liberacion Nacional* (FMLN) (original language). Sometimes claims operations in the name of its individual component groups.

Sponsors Nicaragua, Cuba, the USSR, and Vietnam. Various "solidarity" and fund-raising support groups throughout Latin America, Europe, and North America.

Political Objectives/Target Audiences
- Create and sustain a war of attrition against the elected Government of El Salvador to cause its destruction and replacement by a leftist, pro-Cuban, pro-Soviet, anti-US state.

The emblem of the Farabundo Marti Popular Liberation Forces, one of five insurgent groups under the umbrella of the Farabundo Marti National Liberation Front.

- Frustrate US support of the Salvadoran Government and stimulate domestic US opposition to policies through periodic attacks on American military personnel in El Salvador.

Background

The FMLN is the umbrella organization for five insurgent groups that loosely share Marxist-Leninist ideology and a pro-Cuban/pro-Soviet orientation: the People's Revolutionary Army (ERP), the Farabundo Marti Popular Liberation Forces (FPL), the Armed Forces of National Resistance (FARN), the Revolutionary Party of Central American Workers (PRTC), and the Communist Party of El Salvador's Armed Forces of Liberation (FAL). This alliance was promoted by Cuba in 1980 as a means to create a more effective insurgent organization and as a prerequisite for Cuban material support.

The FMLN external headquarters is located near Managua, Nicaragua, but it maintains "political-diplomatic" offices in Panama, Mexico, and Europe. The FMLN receives external support from Communist countries that channel arms and supplies primarily through Nicaragua. FMLN members are trained routinely at camps in Nicaragua and Cuba. Nicaragua and the undefined border region between El Salvador and Honduras are the primary safehaven areas for the FMLN hardcore members. The scope of FMLN activities is broad, including guerrilla warfare in rural regions and coordination with its political arm, the Revolutionary Democratic Front (FDR). The FMLN also resorts to terrorist tactics, especially when its more conventional military resources are weak.

A bridge in El Salvador that FMLN guerrillas destroyed prior to December 1983.

Most of the foreign-supplied weapons used by FMLN elements are US arms that were lost during the Vietnam War and later filtered through Communist channels into Nicaragua. In addition, weapons and ammunition have been captured from the Salvadoran Army and security forces in ambushes or raids on units and on supply facilities.

Operational funding for the FMLN comes from a variety of sources. Most external funding probably comes through Cuba; the USSR and Vietnam also are believed to contribute. Some money is believed to have come from radical Middle Eastern states as well. As with most Latin American groups, the FMLN conducts kidnaping and ransom operations and extorts "taxes" from businesses and private citizens in contested areas. Overseas front or "solidarity" organizations are also an important source of funds.

An FMLN guerrilla with an American-made M-16 rifle guards the path to his camp in the jungles of El Salvador.

A young FMLN guerrilla carries an RPG-2 in El Salvador.

Selected Incident Chronology

January 1977 — Kidnaped a Salvadoran industrialist and killed three of his bodyguards. A ransom of $1 million was paid, but the victim was killed. (ERP)

May 1978 — Held two prominent Salvadoran businessmen and received a ransom of $4.8 million. (ERP and FPL)

May 1979 — Killed the Charge d'Affaires of the Swiss Embassy in an apparently botched kidnaping attempt. (FPL)

November 1980 — Assassinated the chief of the territorial branch of the Defense Ministry, his wife, and two children in an armed assault on their home. (FARN)

March 1981 — Sprayed the US Embassy with automatic weapons fire for several minutes and fired a rocket-propelled grenade into the side of the building. (FPL)

November 1982 — Killed a Japanese businessman in an unsuccessful attempt to kidnap him in San Jose, Costa Rica. (PRTC)

January 1984 — Mined a landing strip in San Miguel Department and blew up a light civilian aircraft.

June 1985 — Machinegunned an outdoor cafe in San Salvador, killing four US Marine security guards and eight civilians of various nationalities. (PRTC)

September 1985 — Kidnaped Inez Duarte Duran, eldest daughter of Jose Napolean Duarte, President of El Salvador.

November 1987 — In San Salvador gunmen kidnaped and later killed the Salvadoran driver for the US Navy Attache, burned the car he was driving, and removed an embassy radio.

Guatemalan National Revolutionary Unity (URNG)

Date Formed 1982.

Estimated Membership An estimated 1,500 guerrillas from various groups. The URNG is a loose coalition of three of the major insurgent groups in Guatemala that have used terrorist tactics — the Revolutionary Organization of the People in Arms (ORPA), the Guerrilla Army of the Poor (EGP), and the Rebel Armed Forces (FAR).

Headquarters Delegations in Mexico City, Havana, and Managua.

Area of Operations Rural Guatemala, with the OPRA in the southwest, the EGP mainly in the northwest highlands, and the FAR in the extreme north in Peten Department.

Leadership Leaders of each group are believed to form the joint leadership of the URNG, including Rodrigo Asturias Amado ("Gaspar Ilom") of the ORPA, Jorge Soto Garcia ("Pablo Monsanto") of the FAR, and Ricardo Ramirez de Leon ("Rolando Moran") of the EGP.

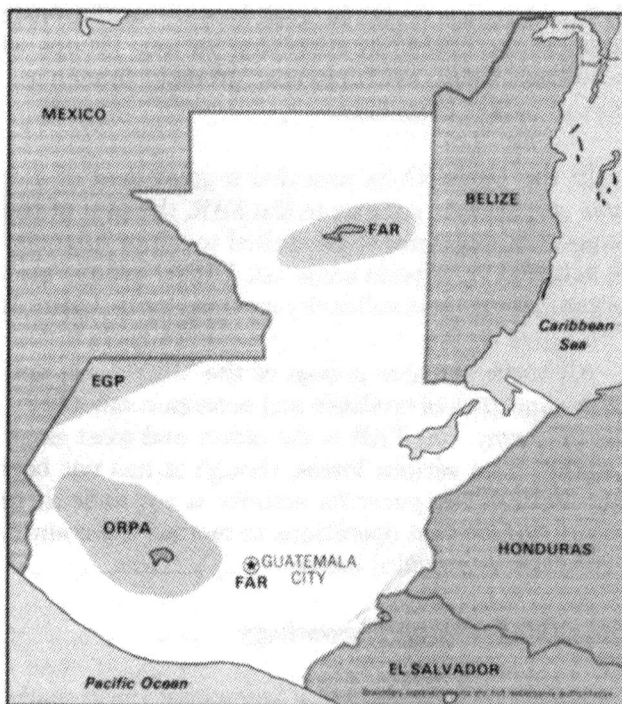

Operating areas of the guerrilla groups that form the loose coalition of the URNG.

Other Names Political arm is known as the Guatemalan Committee for Patriotic Unity (CGUP). Sometimes claims operations in the name of any of its individual component groups.

Sponsors Cuba.

Political Objectives/Target Audiences
- Unify the guerrillas and revolutionary front organizations into a broad coalition to achieve the unity necessary to launch a "people's revolutionary war."
- Defeat the "power of national and foreign wealth and install a patriotic, revolutionary, and democratic people's government."

Background

In 1980, the three groups of the URNG signed a unity agreement that was a precondition for increased Cuban support. The URNG was formalized in Havana in February 1982. As a result, the Government of Guatemala launched a large counteroffensive in an attempt to eliminate the guerrillas' popular support base. By the end of that year, the guerrillas were on the defensive and decreased activity for the next 2 years. In February 1985, they announced "a new stage of military struggle" but showed no evidence of being able to expand their operations.

Cooperation and coordination among the groups is incomplete and irregular. Nonetheless, the URNG stresses joint political-military operations and coordination among its member groups on matters pertaining to territorial responsibilities, tactics, strategy, and external support. Cooperation between groups seems to work best in rural areas, mainly among the ORPA and the FAR. Cuba has assisted the URNG by supplying various groups with Western-made weapons such as assault rifles, recoilless rifles, machineguns, grenade launchers, and mortars, as well as Chinese-made Type-56 RPG-2 rocket launchers.

In the 1960s, Cuba provided a great deal of aid, including weapons, training, logistic, political, and propaganda support to the FAR, the first of the Guatemalan groups to be formed. Recent Cuban support is suspected to be limited to minor financial aid for black market arms purchases. Nicaragua is believed to provide some aid. URNG groups also have ties with various Latin American terrorist organizations and solidarity movements in Latin America, Canada, the United States, and Europe.

All three member groups of the URNG are anti-US and have taken part in operations such as assassinations of civilians and economic sabotage, though most of their activities have been directed at the Army. The FAR is the oldest and most established of the organizations and seems to recover rapidly from serious losses, though it has not been as severely threatened as have the ORPA and the EGP. When guerrilla activity is too difficult to undertake, the FAR seems the most willing to resort to terrorist operations to remind the country that it still exists. A separate list of the FAR's activities is provided below.

Selected Incident Chronology

December 1983 — Hurled a fragmentation grenade at the Salvadoran Embassy in Guatemala City, causing material damage only.

January 1984 — Attacked the official residence of junta leader General Oscar Mejia Victores with machineguns and grenade launchers.

January 1985 — Occupied four towns in El Peten Department during a 3-day period and destroyed a Government vehicle transporting road construction matrials.

October 1985 — Blew up a light aircraft when it tried to land on a mined airstrip of the Panama Farm in Suchitepquez Department, killing the Norwegian Consul in Guatemala.

FAR Attacks

January 1968 — Machinegunned and killed the head of the US Military Mission and the US Naval Attache in Guatemala City. Two other members of the US Military Mission were wounded in the attack.

August 1968 — Assassinated US Ambassador John Gordon Mein on a Guatemala City street after he resisted an apparent kidnaping attempt.

March 1979 — Assassinated an industrialist/landowner in Guatemala City who was the manager of two US-owned enterprises in Huehuetenango.

February 1985 — Occupied seven villages and terrorized a US oil company camp in El Peten Department.

July 1985 — Occupied the camp of a foreign oil company, two towns, and two highway sections. Clashed with Army troops in northern El Peten.

February 1986 — Occupied the Hispanoil oil-drilling camp in El Peten and carried out sabotage actions.

March 1986 — Occupied the Chinaja oil well in Alta Verapaz Department and carried out sabotage actions.

May 1986 — Occupied several towns, sabotaged a pipeline, and attacked an Army company in El Peten.

Lorenzo Zelaya Popular Revolutionary Forces (FPR-LZ)

Date Formed 1978; first operations conducted in 1980.

Estimated Membership 150-300.

Headquarters Tegucigalpa, San Pedro Sula.

Area of Operations Tegucigalpa and San Pedro Sula, and rural northern and central Honduras.

Leadership In question since leader Efrain Duarte Salgado was rumored to have cooperated with the Government while under arrest in 1983.

Other Names *Fuerzas Populares Revolucionarias Lorenzo Zelaya* (original language); sometimes may operate under the name Froylan Turcios Command and Bayardo Paguada Movement.

Sponsors Support, possibly including training, from Nicaragua and Cuba; links with Salvadoran Farabundo Marti National Liberation Front.

Political Objectives/Target Audiences
- Carry out war on US "imperialism" and its allies in Honduras, to include US Embassy and Peace Corps buildings, US military personnel, and US companies.
- Carry out terrorist activities against Latin American embassies.
- Because of close association with the Nicaraguan Sandinistas, serve as Sandinista leverage by threatening retaliation for Honduran support of US policy initiatives toward Nicaragua.

Background

The FPR-LZ is a violently anti-US Marxist-Leninist terrorist organization that first came to public attention in 1980. The group has confined its terrorist activity to Honduras.

FPR-LZ spokesmen have stated publicly that its members have received training in both Cuba and Nicaragua. The purpose of the training was to revive the Honduran guerrilla movement, which Government forces initially crushed in 1983. While in Nicaragua, the group also engaged in action against anti-Sandinista rebels.

Selected Incident Chronology

October 1980 — Strafed the US Embassy Annex in Tegucigalpa with automatic weapons fire and exploded a bomb at the Chilean Embassy.

September 1981 — Ambushed, with automatic weapons, five members of a US Mobile Training Team and exploded a time bomb on the second floor of the National Assembly building.

April 1982 — Raked the US Ambassador's suite on the second floor of the US Embassy in Tegucigalpa with submachinegun fire and threw bombs in front of the Chilean, Peruvian, and Argentine Embassies. FRP-LZ members also hijacked a commercial airliner in Honduras and were allowed to leave for Cuba, without the hostages, after agreeing to the Government's terms.

August 1982 — Exploded time bombs at the offices of two US companies, one Salvadoran company, and the British Embassy.

November 1982 — Exploded time bombs in subsidiaries of the US Castle and Cook Company.

March 1983 — Attacked the Guatemalan Consulate in Tegucigalpa to protest Guatemala's execution of a Honduran terrorist.

March 1987 — Believed to be responsible for a bombing at the home of highly visible Nicaraguan resistance representatives in Tegucigalpa; claimed credit under the name Froylan Turcios Command.

April 1987 — Exploded time bomb in a department store in downtown Tegucigalpa, injuring one passerby.

19th of April Movement (M-19)

Date Formed 19 April 1970 (formation generated by 1970 electoral defeat of the National Popular Alliance political party). First operation claimed in 1974.

Estimated Membership 1,000.

Headquarters Cali, Colombia.

Area of Operations M-19 has two main rural fronts in Colombia: a Southern Front in Putumayo Department (Province) and a Western Front in Caldas, Cauca, Valle del Cauca, Quindio, and Tolima Departments. M-19 also operates in Antioquia. An urban infrastructure exists in the capital, Bogota.

Leadership Carlos *Pizarro* Leon-Gomez, Antonio Navarro, Otty Patino.

Other Names *Movimiento 19 de Abril* (original language).

Sponsors Cuba, Nicaragua, and, to a lesser degree, Libya.

Political Objectives/Target Audiences
- Claiming a populist orientation, emphasize a struggle by the people against the Colombian "bourgeoisie" and American "imperialism."
- Extort funds from narcotics producers and on occasion cooperate with narcotics dealers in areas or ventures of mutual interest.

Background

The M-19 announced its existence on 17 January 1974 by stealing the sword of Simon Bolivar from a Bogota museum, though the group surfaced as early as 1973, when a group of revolutionaries began raiding banks to finance their attacks on Colombian society. The group took its name from the date of the election defeat in 1970 of former President General Gustavo Rojas Pinilla and adopted 19 April 1970 as its founding date.

The M-19 rapidly expanded in 1977 and 1978 and increased in size, capability, and scope of activities as a result of training received from Argentine Montoneros and Uruguayan Tupamaros as well as in Cuba and possibly Libya.

Although the group primarily recruited middle-class intellectuals and students in its early years, by 1985 the M-19 also was recruiting some peasants. Also that year the M-19 announced that it was transforming itself from a guerrilla group into an "army," together with the Popular Liberation Army (EPL) and the Workers' Self-Defense Movement (ADO). After suffering serious losses in clashes with Government forces, the terrorists seized Bogota's Palace of Justice on 6 November 1985.

M-19 activities include occupations of and attacks on towns as well as attacks on army garrisons and high-level military and police officials. The group also engages in fund-raising kidnapings of wealthy businessmen or employees of foreign companies. It has hijacked two commercial jetliners, a cargo plane, and a civilian helicopter.

The M-19 has conducted anti-US terrorist actions, including killing US citizen Chester Bitterman, kidnaping a US mining engineer, and making threats against the US Ambassador.

In addition to kidnaping for ransom, the M-19 obtains some funds through drug-related activities. In 1980, Cuba apparently arranged an arms shipment to the M-19 through Jaime Guillot Lara, a Colombian drug smuggler, although no further operations of this type are known to have occurred. Since 1984, there have been several reports of the group extorting money from narcotics growers. Revenues from drug-related activities complement the M-19's fund-raising through kidnapings, robberies, and external supporters, although there are indications that the group continues to suffer financial shortages.

The M-19 reportedly has ties with many active and dormant Latin American terrorist organizations, including the Uruguayan Tupamaros and the Ecuadorean AVC, as well as groups in El Salvador, Costa Rica, Peru, Guatemala, and Venezuela. M-19 guerrillas also are loosely allied with other Colombian groups such as the Popular Liberation Army (EPL), the National Liberation Army (ELN), the Patria Libre, and the Workers' Revolutionary Party (PRT) under the National Guerrilla Coordinator (CNG), which excludes the Revolutionary Armed Forces of Colombia (FARC). The M-19 also joined in the Simon Bolivar Guerrilla Coordinator, a FARC-led loose alliance formed in 1987. In April 1984, the M-19 announced an alliance with Spain's Basque Fatherland and Liberty separatists for training and mutual assistance.

Many guerrillas probably receive basic training at camps in Colombia and reportedly from Cuba, Nicaragua, and Libya as well. Documents captured in May 1981 indicated that 300 M-19 guerrillas were trained in Cuba in 1980. Cuba also provided the M-19 with weapons during its formative years. Some guns used in the Palace of Justice seizure indicate Nicaragua also may supply some materiel. Currently, many of the M-19's weapons probably are acquired through purchase abroad.

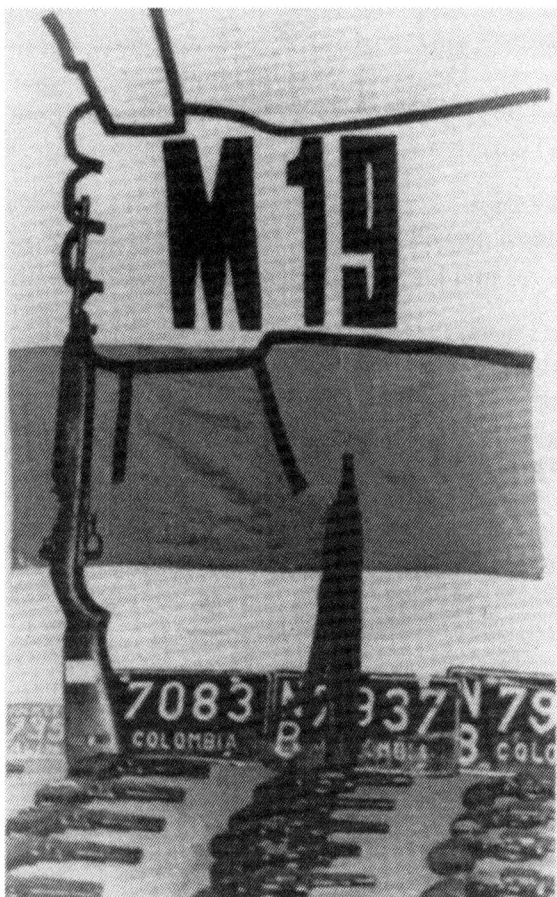

Part of an M-19 arms cache uncovered by Colombian police in Bogota in November 1985.

Two M-19 guerrillas with Czechoslovak Model 25 submachinegun (left) and Israeli Uzi (right).

The M-19 has suffered a series of setbacks since the November 1985 Palace of Justice attack, including the loss of several top leaders. However, the M-19's urban unit in Bogota became active again in late 1987 to early 1988.

Selected Incident Chronology

February 1980 — Seized the Dominican Republic Embassy in Bogota, taking 80 hostages, including the ambassadors from the US and 13 Latin American, European, and Middle Eastern countries. After 61 days, the terrorists flew to Cuba on a Cubana Airlines jet with 11 hostages. Their demands for a $10 million ransom and the release of 28 "political prisoners" were not met.

Colombian M-19 guerrillas held 32 hostages at the Embassy of the Dominican Republic in February 1980.

January-March 1981 — Kidnaped US citizen Chester Allen Bitterman in Bogota and demanded the withdrawal from Colombia of the US Summer Institute of Linguistics, Bitterman's employer. The terrorists executed Bitterman on 7 March 1981 after their demands were not met.

January 1982 — Hijacked a Colombian Aerotal 727 commercial jetliner on a flight between Bogota and Medellin. The hijackers demanded and received a plane to fly to Havana.

April 1983 — Exploded a high-powered bomb in the building housing the Honduran Embassy in Bogota, seriously wounding the Honduran Consul.

March 1984 — Staged three simultaneous attacks on military and police installations and banks in the town of Florencia.

August 1985 — Participated in the kidnaping of Ecuadorean banker Nahim Isaias from his home near Guayaquil, Ecuador. He and his Ecuadorean AVC and Colombian M-19 captors were killed in the Ecuadorean police rescue attempt.

October 1985 — Intercepted the automobile of Army Commander General Rafael Samudio Molina in Bogota, but fled after a firefight with the general's escorts.

November 1985 — Seized Bogota's Palace of Justice and took almost 500 hostages, including many members of the Supreme Court and the Council of State. Security forces counterattacked, freeing 300-400 of the hostages and killing 15-18 of the terrorists. By the end of the incident, 50 hostages, including 11 Supreme Court justices, were killed, as well as 11 members of the security forces and all of the remaining terrorists.

Two female members of the M-19 before the fatal assault on the Palace of Justice building in November 1985.

December 1985 — Attempted to ambush the National Police Subdirector, General Guillermo Medino Sanchez, in his car.

March 1986 — Occupied San Bernardino Seminary for 24 hours and attempted to attack a police post in the resort town of Juanchito.

June 1986 — Attempted to assassinate Minister of Government Jaime Castro as he drove to work.

July 1986 — Stole 1.6 million pesos from a bank in Bogota, wounding two civilians in the attack.

September 1986 — Attempted kidnaping of a businessman in Bucaramanga. The Army rescued the victim and captured all the guerrillas.

October 1986 — Stole $690,000 in jewelery from a store in Medellin (the owner of the store was kidnaped and killed in February 1986).

November 1986 — Attacked the Cordova Museum in Santuario and stole several items. Police pursued the attackers, recovered the items, and killed one guerrilla while capturing two.

September 1987 — Took over the Bogota newspaper *Diario 5 p.m.* and published a propaganda piece.

Macheteros (Machete Wielders)

Date Formed 1978.

Estimated Membership Unknown.

Headquarters Unknown

Area of Operations Puerto Rico.

Leadership Unknown.

Other Names *Ejercito Popular de Boricua* (EPB), Boricua Popular Army. (*Boricua* refers to rural inland Puerto Ricans.)

Sponsors None known.

Political Objectives/Target Audiences
- Wage a terrorist war against "US colonialist imperialism."
- Create public support for creation of a separate Puerto Rican nation.

Background

The Macheteros are a tightly organized and extremely violent Puerto Rican separatist group that has targeted primarily US military personnel and Puerto Rican police. The group has tight internal security procedures and precisely executes its attacks.

The Macheteros appear to be fiercely dedicated to total Puerto Rican independence. Nothing short of that is likely to cause them to cease terrorist operations. The stated position of the group is that they have "declared war" on the United States.

Direct ties of the Macheteros to other groups operating in Latin America have not been established. There is apparent cooperation with another Puerto Rican separatist group called the Organization of Volunteers for the Puerto Rican Revolution. The two have made joint claims following some attacks. The Macheteros probably also have links to the Armed Forces of National Liberation, a Puerto Rican separatist group that has conducted anti-US attacks for over three decades.

Robberies and thefts evidently provide a major source of funds. The Macheteros also may receive donations from ideological backers.

Selected Incident Chronology

August 1978 — Killed a policeman during a robbery.

December 1979 — Killed two sailors in an attack on a US Navy bus.

March 1980 — Fired on a bus carrying three ROTC instructors from the University of Puerto Rico.

January 1981 — Destroyed eight aircraft and damaged two others in a carefully executed multiple bombing attack on the Air National Guard airfield. Damage was estimated at $40 million.

May 1982 — Killed one sailor and wounded three others in an ambush outside a San Juan nightclub.

September 1983 — Robbed a Wells Fargo armored truck depot in Hartford, Connecticut. The $7.2 million heist was the second largest in US history.

October 1983 — Fired an antitank rocket into the new Federal Building in San Juan to protest US rescue operations in Grenada.

January 1985 — Fired an antitank rocket into the Federal Courthouse in San Juan.

November 1985 — Shot and wounded a US Army recruiting officer in an ambush while he was on his way to work.

October 1986 — Placed some 10 explosive devices at military and military-related facilities across the island.

November 1986 — Placed a bomb at a National Guard building in old San Juan.

December 1986 — Bombed a vehicle at the National Guard Center at Yauco.

Manuel Rodriguez Patriotic Front (FPMR)

Date Formed 1983.

Estimated Membership 500-1,000.

Headquarters Santiago.

Area of Operations Urban areas of Chile.

Leadership Unknown.

Other Names *Frente Patriotico Manuel Rodriguez* (original language).

Sponsors Associated with the Chilean Communist Party and probably receives some assistance from Cuba and elsewhere.

Political Objectives/Target Audiences
- Bring about the downfall of the Pinochet regime in Chile through a terrorist campaign designed to provoke greater Government repression and anti-Government sentiment. Strongly influence, if not actually lead, a subsequent government toward leftist, anti-US, and pro-Soviet policies.
- Pressure US interests to leave Chile through periodic attacks on business or government facilities.

Background

The FPMR, which takes its name from a 19th century Chilean revolutionary executed by Spanish authorities, is a relatively new but very active urban terrorist group. Not a great deal is known about its structure, but judging from its activities to date, it probably is relatively well organized and equipped.

The FPMR is closely related with the Chilean Communist Party and has links to Cuba and other Communist countries, especially for training and weapons supply.

In early 1985, FPMR spokesman Daniel Huerta said that the purpose of the group was to conduct exclusively urban terrorist operations. The structure of the organization would stress a cellular grouping of militants, who would earn their status by demonstrating "selflessness, sacrifice, combat ability, solidarity, and moral and military qualities."

The FPMR has an impressive arsenal that includes remotely detonated bombs and a variety of small arms, rocket-propelled grenades, and handgrenades. Several weapons caches have been discovered by authorities, but attacks continue, indicating sufficient sources of supplies. The group's operations have been primarily bombings, although it also has carried out kidnapings and assassinations. The FPMR was responsible for the nearly successful assassination attempt against President Pinochet in September 1986.

Although the FPMR has been most active in Santiago, it has conducted operations in at least eight other cities. It frequently uses the mass media in its campaigns and sometimes seizes a radio station to broadcast its propaganda.

Selected Incident Chronology

March 1984 — Carried out simultaneous bombing attacks in Santiago, Valparaiso, Concepcion, and San Antonio. Considerable property damage was done, seven people were injured, and dozens were arrested in riots that followed.

April 1984 — Bombed a Santiago subway station, wounding 20.

August 1984 — Bombed the US Cultural Center in Valparaiso and two US businesses in Santiago as part of a series of bomb attacks throughout central Chile.

December 1984 — Kidnaped the assistant director of a pro-Government newspaper.

March 1985 — Bombed offices of two US banks, Citibank and Republic National, along with several Chilean facilities in Santiago and other cities.

January 1986 — Believed responsible for the bombing of the US-Chilean Cultural Institute in Vina del Mar.

April 1986 — Blacked out major portions of central Chile in an attack on electrical power facilities.

April 1986 — Detonated a bomb by the perimeter wall of the US Ambassador's residence in Santiago.

August 1986 — Kidnaped a Chilean Army colonel — the first abduction of a high-ranking military officer since the 1973 coup. He was released 3 days later.

August 1986 — Arms caches containing more than 3,100 weapons of US and other manufacture were discovered in the area of Copiapo and Santiago. Witnesses presented by the Chilean Government indicate the weapons were smuggled ashore from Cuban fishing trawlers off the coast of Chile.

September 1986 — Attempted to assassinate Chilean President Pinochet. Weapons used were of the same type found in the arms caches.

November 1986 — Conducted a series of dynamite attacks against power lines, blacking out the main cities in central and southern Chile.

February-March 1987 — Set off dynamite explosions at pylons and towers of the national high-voltage power network, blacking out areas of Santiago, Valparaiso, and Vina del Mar. March incident occurred as President Pinochet spoke on radio and television.

April 1987 — Santiago police deactivated a powerful bomb discovered in the office of the prosecutor who tried 14 FPMR members and held them for 5 months.

April 1987 — Gunmen briefly seized control of eight radio stations in four cities with the objective of playing a clandestine broadcast, ending a self-proclaimed truce during the visit of Pope John Paul II. An off-duty guard was killed attempting to stop the gunmen's escape.

May 1987 — Detonated bombs that destroyed four high-tension towers, resulting in a general power outage at Copiapo and Valdivia.

June 1987 — Conducted a machinegun and bomb attack at a Santiago printing company, injuring three. Two other incidents that day at two National Intelligence Center barracks caused little damage and no injuries.

June 1987 — Ambushed police patrol cars in Santiago with machineguns and firebombs. These separate evening attacks wounded two policemen and several passersby.

June 1987 — Staged several machinegun, bomb, and firebomb attacks against police, pro-Government media, and Government offices in Santiago and Talca, causing five injuries and costly damage. Although the FPMR attempted to use rockets in three incidents, two were deactivated before being remotely fired and one failed to explode when triggered. (The June attacks may have been retaliatory for the killing of 12 FPMR members by security agents on June 16.)

July 1987 — Four gunmen shot and killed a policeman waiting for a bus on a Santiago street. (Possible FPMR responsibility.)

September 1987 — Kidnaped Chilean Army LTC Carlos Carreno in Santiago. He was released in December 1987 in Sao Paulo, Brazil.

Movement of the Revolutionary Left (MIR)

Date Formed 1965.

Estimated Membership 500.

Headquarters Havana, Cuba, and Santiago, Chile.

Area of Operations Chile.

Leadership Andres Pascal Allende, Hernan Aguilo Donoso, Manuel Cabieses Donoso, Nelson Gutierrez.

Other Names *Movimiento de la Izquierda Revolucionaria* (original language).

Sponsors Cuba.

Political Objectives/Target Audiences

- Conduct terrorist actions in an attempt to provoke the Government to take repressive measures that will alienate the general public.
- Establish a Marxist state in Chile.
- Conduct occasional acts of terrorism against US targets to force American interests out of Chile and to exert social and economic pressure on the Chilean (Pinochet) Government.

Background

The MIR was formed by far left university students in 1965. Very shortly thereafter, they made a concerted shift to Castroite views and began an association with the Cuban regime. When authorities began to zero in on top leader Andres *Pascal* Allende, he fled to Cuba, where he currently runs the MIR headquarters. Cuba has provided military training to MIR members, along with other support.

During the Popular Unity government (1970-73) of Marxist President Salvador Allende, the MIR attempted to push Allende into taking more radical steps to advance the revolution by organizing peasant land seizures and factory takeovers. MIR militants also spoke of recruiting militias from urban factory workers.

After the 1973 coup, the MIR resisted the consolidation of military rule more actively than any other group in Chile and was strongly repressed. Many MIR leaders, including Miguel Enriquez, the MIR chief, were killed in shootouts with the military, while others fled abroad. The political wing of the organization collapsed, and the MIR became a purely guerrilla operation, albeit ineffective.

After the social unrest of 1983, the MIR rebounded somewhat, both in its military-terrorist activity and politically. While the hardcore terrorist faction of the MIR is small, its political wing is larger.

To help finance its terrorist operations, the MIR has relied increasingly on bank robberies. Captured equipment has included automatic weapons and antitank rockets. The group also has the ability to build a variety of bombs.

Selected Incident Chronology

February 1979 — Bombed the US-Chile Cultural Institute in Santiago, causing considerable damage.

July 1980 — Assassinated the director of the Chilean Army Intelligence School and his chauffeur in a machinegun attack.

November 1981 — Killed three members of the Investigative Police as they stood in front of the home of the chief minister of the Presidential staff.

August 1983 — Machinegunned and killed the Intendente (military governor) of the Santiago Metropolitan Region, his driver, and his bodyguard in a well-coordinated assault.

October-November 1983 — Bombed four US-associated targets in a 10-day period.

November 1984 — Detonated a large car bomb outside a police station in Valparaiso.

March 1985 — Claimed responsibility for the deaths of two men who were attempting to defuse a bomb in Concepcion.

February 1986 — Injured 16 police by detonating a car bomb near their bus; one later died of his injuries.

May 1986 — Threw sulphuric acid into a bus, seriously injuring six people, including two children.

October 1986 — Attacked a police station in Limache with gunfire, seriously wounding five. One policeman later died of his wounds.

June 1988 — Conducted a series of four bombing incidents in Santiago, Chile, all at various bank branch offices around the city. No injuries occurred, but the attacks caused serious damage.

National Liberation Army (ELN)

Date Formed July 1964.

Estimated Membership Less than 1,000.

Headquarters Colombia.

Area of Operations Primarily the north and northeastern parts of the country, near the Venezuelan border; expanding into the central region.

Leadership Manuel *Perez* Martinez and Nicolas *Rodrigues* Bautista ("Dario").

Other Names *Ejercito de Liberacion Nacional* (original language).

Sponsors Believed to be assisted by Cuba.

Political Objectives/Target Audiences
- Pro-Castro, anti-US, and Marxist-Leninist.
- Also anticapitalist and anti-"national bourgeoisie."
- Seek "the conquest of power for the popular classes" along with nationalizations, expropriations, and agrarian reform.

Background

The ELN is a political-military organization drawing members from a wide variety of Colombians, from students and intellectuals to peasants and middle-class workers. It has several factions and fronts, to include the "Camilo Torres Restrepo," the "Jose Antonio Galan," and the "Domingo Lain Sanz," as well as the "Simon Bolivar" faction, which opposes the hardliners in the ELN. The ELN is the one Colombian insurgent group that refused to agree to a truce with the Government in 1984.

The ELN forms part of the National Guerrilla Coordinator (CNG) and the recently formed Simon Bolivar Guerrilla Coordinator (SBGC).

Actions undertaken by the ELN include kidnapings of wealthy ranchers and industrialists; assassinations of military officers, labor leaders, and peasants; armed robberies; bombings; raids on isolated villages; assaults on police posts and army patrols (primarily to obtain weapons); and occupations of radio stations and newspaper offices. Most recently the ELN has concentrated its efforts on attacking petroleum pipelines and facilities, damaging Colombia's economic infrastructure and investment climate.

In the early part of 1988, the ELN has been the most active terrorist group in Colombia. The arsenal of the ELN includes explosives, small arms, semiautomatic weapons, grenades, and antitank rockets.

Selected Incident Chronology

January 1980 — Kidnaped an Englishwoman and her son from their farm in Cesar Department and demanded a $300,000 ransom.

January 1982 — Kidnaped a diplomat of the Honduran Embassy in Bogota to protest alleged Honduran interference in domestic affairs of Nicaragua and El Salvador.

July 1983 — Claimed responsibility for a series of dynamite attacks in Colombia as part of "Operation Free Central America." The Salvadoran Consulate in Medellin and two local police offices in the suburb of Aranjuez were the targets.

November 1983 — Kidnaped the Colombian President's brother but returned him unharmed 15 days later, after Fidel Castro intervened.

May 1984 — Six ELN members raided a gold mine near the northwestern town of Segovia and seized almost $90,000.

June 1985 — Ambushed and killed eight policemen patrolling near the Venezuelan border.

November 1986 — Bombed a dredge in the Nechi River in Colombia and temporarily paralyzed gold production in the area. Also killed an Army sergeant in an ambush on a patrol in northwest Colombia, attacked an oil camp, and kidnaped two people in northeast Colombia.

December 1986 — Made numerous raids against US-associated oil production subsidiaries, destroying machinery and stealing explosives.

January-June 1987 — Continued to target Colombia's oil production by blowing up sections of pipeline and attacking oil camps. During this period, the ELN may have attained the leadership position within the National Guerrilla Coordinator (CNG), replacing the M-19.

April-August 1987 — Bombed oil operation locations and US-Colombian targets, causing considerable property damage.

June 1987 — Ambushed Venezuelan National Guard unit on antinarcotics mission near Colombian border.

September 1987 — Attacked Venezuelan Army border outpost to capture weapons.

October 1987 — Bombed three Mormon churches in Boyaca and a naval facility in Barrancabermeja.

November 1987 — Killed 17 policemen and 4 soldiers in separate ambushes in northeastern and southern Colombia.

Popular Liberation Army (EPL)

Date Formed 1967.

Estimated Membership 600-800.

Headquarters Colombia.

Area of Operations Primarily Antioquia and Cordoba Departments (Provinces), Colombia.

Leadership Jairo Clavo ("Ernesto Rodas") — killed by police in February 1987; Francisco Caraballo; Javier Robles.

Other Names *Ejercito Popular de Liberacion* (original language).

Sponsors No external sponsors known; armed wing of the Colombian Communist Party — Marxist-Leninist (PCC-ML).

Political Objectives/Target Audiences
- Conduct war of liberation directed at the "Colombian bourgeoisie."
- Emphasize peasant struggle of Maoist orientation.

Background

The EPL emerged in late 1967 as a result of Maoist influence on Marxist-Leninist thinking. It is the armed branch of the miniscule pro-Peking PCC-ML.

Throughout the 1970s, the EPL retained its ideological link with Peking, despite its diminutive size in comparison with other active Colombian groups. During the late 1970s, the EPL was responsible for occasional sabotage attacks, kidnapings, bank robberies, and bombings. Beginning in early 1987, the EPL began to develop a rural campaign in the Uraba region, making it one of the two most consistently active guerrilla zones in the country.

The EPL, the National Liberation Army (ELN), the M-19, and two other small groups compose the National Guerrilla Coordinator (CNG). The CNG structure was largely overcome by the advent of the Simon Bolivar Guerrilla Coordinator (SBGC), which the EPL also joined.

The Maoist ideological stance continues to appeal to a small circle of university-based intellectuals who provide aid to the terrorist movement. The group remains active despite damaging arrests and retains influence in Bogota, Convencion, Medellin, Cali, Popayan, Pereira, and Tierra Alta.

Members of the EPL embarking on a rural propaganda campaign.

Selected Incident Chronology

December 1982 — Kidnaped a wealthy landowner in northeast Colombia and demanded a $2 million ransom.

September 1983 — Raided a payroll transport vehicle in Itaqui and stole $120,000, which was recovered shortly thereafter.

January 1984 — Attacked the town of Sabana Larga, Antioquia Department; killed six policemen, burned the mayor's office, and looted the Agrarian Credit Fund and stores.

March 1984 — Executed eight peasants as Army informers and killed the police chief of a small town in northwest Colombia.

June 1984 — Assaulted a police station in downtown Medellin with machineguns, killing one policeman and wounding four others. The terrorists later bombed the building.

November 1985 — Broke a ceasefire agreement with the Government, attacking a small town in northeast Colombia, killing four people.

December 1985 — Kidnaped two US employees of Bechtel Corporation; one died in captivity in May 1986, and the other was later released.

June 1986 — Conducted a bombing attack against the Colombian-Soviet Friendship Institute in Medellin as reprisal against the Revolutionary Armed Forces of Colombia (FARC) for clashes between FARC and EPL forces.

June 1986 — Bombed the Honduran Consul's residence in Medellin, seriously injuring her.

February 1987 — Exploded a bomb near the Chamber of Commerce building in Bogota; a passerby was wounded.

May 1987 — Kidnaped a delegate of the National Voter Registry in Caramelo. Freed him later but confiscated the voter list, preventing elections in the town.

October 1987 — Briefly occupied a Bogota radio station to broadcast anti-Government slogans.

Revolutionary Armed Forces of Colombia (FARC)

Date Formed 1966.

Estimated Membership About 4,000-5,000 armed guerrillas in 35-40 fronts.

Headquarters La Uribe, Meta Department.

Area of Operations Colombia.

Leadership Manuel *Marulanda* Velez (AKA Pedro Antonio Marin and Tirofijo), Jacobo Arenas.

Other Names *Fuerzas Armadas Revolucionarias de Colombia* (original language).

Political Objectives/Target Audiences

Through a two-pronged strategy combining insurgent/terrorist operations with participation in the legitimate political process, the FARC and its political front, the Patriotic Union (UP), have these objectives:
- Overthrow the established order in Colombia and replace it with a leftist and anti-American regime.
- Create a "broad antimonopoly and anti-imperialist front" and unite leftwing parties and organizations into a political movement.
- Force US and other "imperialist" interests out of Colombia.

Background

The FARC is probably the largest, best-trained and equipped, and most effective insurgent organization in Colombia and in South America.

The FARC is pro-Soviet, pro-Cuban, and anti-American, and proclaims dedication to Marxist-Leninist ideology. The FARC often is described as the "military" apparatus of the Moscow-line Communist Party of Colombia (PCC), although the FARC and the PCC frequently downplay their connections.

Since May 1984, the FARC has nominally observed a cease-fire accord with the Government of Colombia, but it has not given up its "armed struggle." During the cease-fire, FARC forces have carried out terrorist actions, such as extortion, kidnapings, and killings, as well as attacks against military units. The FARC's attempts at peace appear to be a method for preparing its political path, inhibiting pressure from Colombian security forces, and allowing the FARC time to regroup. The FARC continues to use its claim of observing the truce to buy time, all the while conducting ambushes, town seizures, extortion, etc.

The FARC's leadership is largely disaffected middle- and upper-class intellectuals, although it recruits from, and attempts to appeal to, the peasant population. The FARC also has received support from other elements of Colombian society, including workers, students, and radical priests. FARC popularity has been undermined by the occasional practice of kidnaping peasants and killing them as collaborators and traitors if they do not cooperate. The FARC has attempted to strengthen its influence over other insurgent factions by leading the recent efforts to establish the national Simon Bolivar Guerrilla Coordinator (SBGC), which includes all major Colombian insurgent groups.

Within the last 3 years, the FARC has spawned a political movement and a radical dissident faction. The Patriotic Union (UP) is the leftist political front that is pursuing FARC interests through electoral and political processes. Both the UP and the FARC recently increased activities in preparation for the March 1988 national mayoral elections. The Ricardo Franco Front (RFF) broke away from FARC in March 1984 over differences in tactics. The RFF became an active terrorist group in its own right, but has been relatively dormant in the last year.

The FARC has a closer relationship with Colombian narcotics traffickers than do other Colombian insurgent groups. The relationship appears strongest in areas where coca production and FARC operational strongholds overlap. In local instances, in return for FARC protection of narcotics interests, the guerrillas have received money to purchase weapons and supplies. There are continuing reports, and strong indications, that various FARC fronts actually are involved in processing cocaine.

Money from the narcotics trade supplements FARC revenues from kidnapings, extortion, and robberies. The group's arsenals include a wide variety of Western-made rifles, carbines, submachineguns, pistols, revolvers, handgrenades, and mortars. The weapons are captured, stolen, bought on the black market, or shipped from other countries.

Selected Incident Chronology

February 1977 — Kidnaped a US Peace Corps volunteer during an attack on La Macarena. The volunteer was released 3 years later after a $250,000 ransom was paid.

August 1980 — Kidnaped a US citizen from his banana plantation in central Colombia. He was released 3 months later after a $125,000 ransom was paid.

April 1983 — Kidnaped a US citizen from her farm in southern Meta Department and demanded a sizable ransom.

August 1983 — Kidnaped a US citizen who was a ranchowner in Meta Department. The victim was released 18 January 1984 after payment of a large ransom.

February 1985 — Bombed seven businesses in a midnight attack in Medellin, including IBM, General Telephone and Electronics, Union Carbide, and Xerox.

August 1985 — Kidnaped 4 engineers and 30 workers of a construction farm in Huila Department after the company refused an $80,000 extortion demand.

October 1985 — Kidnaped four missionaries in the eastern plains. The FARC met with a delegation from the Government's Peace Commission and agreed to free the victims.

December 1985 — Kidnaped a Venezuelan rancher, who was rescued by Venezuelan police in February 1986 in the Arauca River region. The six kidnapers died in the clash.

January 1986 — Demanded $100 million from Shell Oil Company to continue operating in the middle Magaleas valley, but the firm suspended its operations in the region instead of meeting the demand.

February 1986 — Attacked the town of Rio Sucio in northern Choco Department, killing one policeman and wounding another. Destroyed three buildings.

August 1986 — Conducted a bomb attack in Nencoon; police bomb squad members killed while attempting to disarm a bomb.

Before and after photographs of an unsuccessful attempt by police bomb squad members to disarm a bomb planted by guerrillas in Nencoon, Colombia, on 7 August 1986.

November 1986 — The remains of some 100 men, women, and children were found in a mass grave in Turbo; they were thought to have been murdered by the FARC.

April 1987 — Kidnaped seven employees of a rancher in Bogota; one body found later.

June 1987 — In violation of the truce, the FARC ambushed an Army road-building crew in Caqueta Department, killing 27. President Barco then declared the truce "broken" with the FARC in that and any other area where the FARC attacks Government forces.

December 1987 — Approximately 50 FARC members attacked the town of Gaitania, killing 2 policemen and wounding 5; the FARC employed grenades, automatic weapons, light antitank rockets, and molotov cocktails.

January 1988 — Two hundred miles southwest of Bogota, 40 FARC members hijacked a helicopter operated by a Colombian air charter service and chartered by two Western oil companies.

Ricardo Franco Front (RFF)

Date Formed Became an independent faction in March 1984.

Estimated Membership 100.

Headquarters Valle del Cauca Department (Province), Colombia.

Area of Operations Primarily terrorist operations in Bogota, as well as activity in other parts of southwest Colombia.

Leadership Jose Fedor *Rey* Alvarez (AKA Javier Delgado).

Other Names *Frente Ricardo Franco* (original language).

Sponsors None known; has participated in National Guerrilla Coordinator (CNG) with other Colombian groups.

Political Objectives/Target Audiences

- Overthrow the established order and form a "people's government" — an objective similar to that of its original parent group, the Revolutionary Armed Forces of Colombia (FARC).
- Oppose US involvement in Colombia: the RFF has demonstrated the strongest anti-American sentiments of the Colombian guerrilla groups, frequently targeting US official and commercial installations in 1984 and 1985, although it has been fairly inactive since then.

Background

In 1984, the RFF grew out of FARC dissidents who were displeased with the FARC program and upset by the FARC's agreement to a truce with the Government. FARC and RFF guerrillas attacked each other on several occasions after their split.

The RFF increased terrorist activities in 1985, at a time when the FARC was trying to pursue political objectives and abide by the truce. The FARC has been blamed for many RFF activities and its credibility damaged because of the former close relationship with the RFF.

Also in 1985, the RFF decided to cooperate with some of Colombia's other terrorist organizations and formalized an agreement to undertake joint actions with the National Liberation Army (ELN), the only major movement at that time opposing the Government truce. The RFF apparently also allied with the M-19 group, on one occasion fighting alongside M-19 for 10 days in Tolima Department.

In December 1985, a bloody purge occurred within the RFF, with as many as 100 RFF members killed and buried in mass graves later uncovered by Colombian security forces. When this information became public, other members of the National Guerrilla Coordinator (CNG), such as the M-19, issued public statements breaking off relations with the RFF. The incident caused serious factionalization within the RFF, and it has been fairly inactive since that time. At present, the RFF could be described more accurately as a bandit group than as a guerrilla organization.

Selected Incident Chronology

May 1984 — Claimed responsibility for bombings at a Honduran airline company that left 2 dead and 11 injured, as well as a smaller bomb at a US diplomatic facility.

January 1985 — Attacked a Bolivar Department village and kidnaped seven people. One policeman was killed and one wounded in the clash.

January 1985 — Bombed the Colombian Labor Ministry.

February 1985 — Placed eight bombs at or near several US company locations in Medellin; killed one and wounded one.

Spring 1985 — Attempted to occupy, with 150 guerrillas, the wealthy Bogota suburb of Cuba. Authorities deactivated 26 bombs set to destroy bridges and police stations in critical parts of the city.

May 1985 — Bombed a bridge, Government buildings, and a police academy.

June 1985 — Shot and seriously wounded a congressman who is also a high-ranking Communist Party member and Executive Secretary of the Colombian Committee for Defense of Human Rights.

June 1985 — Murdered a regional high official of the State Oil Company. He had been kidnaped 5 days before, and a ransom of $105,000 had been demanded.

September 1985 — After 10 days of heavy fighting alongside the M-19 group, both forces withdrew from central and southern Colombia to Tolima Department.

September 1985 — Staged numerous attacks against US and other embassies and multinational company locations. In some cases, advance police warnings minimized the effect and only minor injuries or property damage occurred. At the US Embassy, two small children were paid by persons in a vehicle to place a time bomb at the gates. It was deactivated in time.

Shining Path (SL)

Dated Formed 1969; began terrorist operations in 1980.

Estimated Membership 4,000-5,000.

Headquarters Ayacucho Department.

Area of Operations Peru.

Leadership Manuel Ruben Abimael *Guzman* (AKA President Gonzalo), Julio Cesar *Mezzich*, Carlota *Tello* Cutti (AKA Carla).

Other Names *Sendero Luminoso* (original language).

Sponsors No foreign sponsors known.

Political Objectives/Target Audiences
- Stimulate a "peasant armed struggle" that will lead to overthrow of the current constitutional government and install a leftist, ethnic Indian state by the year 2000.
- Attack US and other "imperialist" targets in an effort to eliminate foreign influence in Peru, embarrass the Peruvian Government, and force it to take repressive measures. The SL also has attacked Soviet and Chinese targets.

Background

The Shining Path is a highly active and violent terrorist/insurgent group that claims a neo-Maoist orientation. Its hope is to create a rural-based insurgency that will sweep into the cities and destroy the current system of government.

The SL developed from an extremist splinter group of the Peruvian Communist Party (PCP). It has tried to radicalize the Marxist-Leninist movement in Peru and feels that the "old, heroic traditions of the Quechua Indians" are the proper elements for a new social/political system. By using names and symbols from the Indian heritage of the rural regions, the SL has been able to attract some support that might not have been drawn to a purely Marxist ideology.

The SL is organized to conduct simultaneous urban terrorism and rural guerrilla warfare. Although it is large and adequately equipped and trained, the group tends to avoid direct conflict with the military unless it can attack with overwhelming force.

Unlike most other Latin American leftist subversive groups, the SL is not believed to have obvious or extensive ties to Cuba or other sponsors. Bank robberies and extortion are the primary sources of funding. The SL imposes a "war tax" that apparently provides a large source of income.

The SL conducts very aggressive indoctrination programs in its rural bases. Its recruiting practices frequently target 12- to 15-year-olds who can be molded into highly motivated, even fanatical activists.

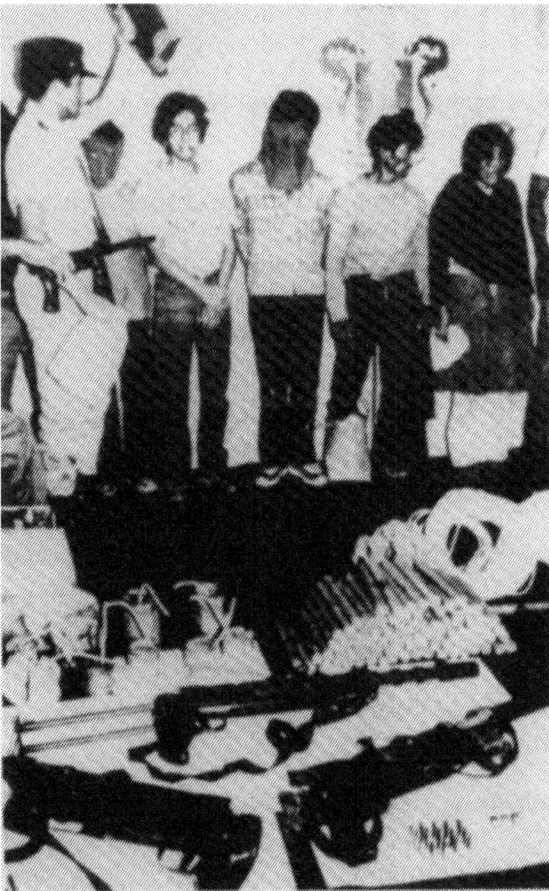

Suspected members of Shining Path and their weapons captured by civil guard.

The SL employs a cellular structure for terrorist operations, and each cell has at least one female member. Women serve as members of assault teams as well as smugglers, intelligence operatives, and messengers.

Particularly gruesome assassinations are a hallmark of the SL. Victims often are ritually mutilated, and the corpses are left on public display. This feature of the SL operations is partly a reflection of an Indian belief that an unmutilated victim's spirit can reveal its killer, and it also magnifies the terror effect of the killings.

Although the SL espouses a rural, peasant revolution, its leadership comes from radical middle-class intellectual circles. The leaders, however, are very skillful at maintaining the image of a "people's movement," thus enhancing the SL's ability to attract support in the rural regions. Nonetheless, if a village demonstrates resistance to an SL takeover, residents frequently are terrorized into cooperation; extermination of the village leadership is not uncommon.

The principal targets of the SL assassination teams are civilian technicians of Government-sponsored civic action projects and local political leaders affiliated with the American Popular Revolutionary Alliance (APRA) political party. Several relatively ambitious development projects cannot get off the ground because the SL assassinates the technicians, destroys works completed, and blows up construction machinery needed to continue work. Economic disruption by the SL also has targeted the railways in an attempt to cripple the major transportation system.

Selected Incident Chronology

August 1981 — Bombed the US Embassy, the Bank of America, the Coca Cola bottler, and a dairy product firm associated with the Carnation Company, all in Lima.

July 1982 — Threw two dynamite bombs at the US Embassy and set off bombs at three private businesses, injuring three people.

May 1983 — Blew up 10 electrical powerline towers in a coordinated attack that blacked out Lima, and set off over 30 bombs during the confusion, causing over $27 million in damage.

October 1983 — Bombed the car of a Lima policeman.

May 1984 — Machinegunned two policemen on duty outside the West German Embassy in Lima, killing one and wounding the other.

August 1984 — Burned an evangelical church run by US missionaries in southeastern Ayacucho Department.

November 1984 — Bombed the US-Peruvian Cultural Institute in Lima.

April 1985 — Shot and critically wounded a former Supreme Court Justice who was serving as president of the National Elections Tribunal.

June 1985 — Allegedly placed a car bomb near the Presidential Palace in Lima.

August 1985 — Bombed a bus at the Chamber of Commerce in Lima.

December 1985 — Set off a bomb in the Lima airport parking lot, killing a child and four other people.

February 1986 — Shot and killed Chupac village mayor Pedro Parades, stole food stored in a church, and threatened to kill the priest.

March 1986 — Assassinated three provincial mayors by shooting them in the head in the town of Chacra Pampas.

Policeman guards bodies killed by the Shining Path in September 1985.

June 1986 — Over 200 alleged SL members killed in a prison riot and the subsequent Government attempt to retake the prison.

June 1986 — Bombed Cuzco-Machu Picchu tourist train, killing 8 (including 1 American) and wounding 40 (including 9 Americans).

July 1986 — Bombed the Soviet Embassy in Lima.

October 1986 — Shot and killed former Navy Minister Admiral Cafferatta.

January 1987 — Shot and killed senior APRA member Carlos Silva.

January 1987 — Attacked Indian Embassy.

February 1987 — Bombed seven banks and burned a textile factory in Lima.

February 1987 — Failed in an attempt to assassinate Peruvian Attorney General; detonated two car bombs near a political rally where President Garcia was speaking.

March 1987 — Conducted an unsuccessful assassination attempt against the Bank of Tokyo general manager.

The results of a car bomb allegedly placed by Shining Path guerrillas near the Presidential Palace in Lima, Peru, in June 1985.

Shining Path terrorists bombed this bus in front of the Chamber of Commerce in Lima, Peru, in August 1985.

March 1987 — Assassinated Peruvian officer in daylight near his home.

April 1987 — Carried out bloody daylight attack against a restaurant near Peruvian Army headquarters, indiscriminately killing military and civilian customers.

April 1987 — Killed two policemen guarding the Huanchac train station in Cuzco.

April 1987 — Assaulted a busload of military and civilian passengers in Huanacavelica, killing 13 people.

April 1987 — Attacked the North Korean Commercial Mission in Lima, injuring at least three people.

May 1987 — Conducted a major series of bombings, blacking out most of Lima. Targets included the Ministries of Agriculture, Labor, and Transportation and Communication.

June 1987 — Attacked an exclusive restaurant in the Monterrico District in Lima. At least one restaurant guard and two attackers were wounded.

July-November 1987 — Staged numerous clashes with security forces supporting narcotics eradication campaign in upper Huallaga valley.

August 1987 — Killed APRA party leader Rodrigo Franco.

September-October 1987 — Detonated car bomb near Congress Building, causing partial blackout in Lima. Killed over 40 civilians in attacks against 2 towns in Tocache Province.

October 1987 — Suspected in assassination of APRA party leader Nelson Pozo.

November 1987 — Suspected in coordinated Lima blackout and attack against Nissan factory, dynamite bombings of Ministries of Health and Justice, and attack against US Embassy.

June 1988 — Two US Agency for International Development subcontractors were killed while traveling near Huancayo, Peru, an area controlled by the SL.

Tupac Amaru Revolutionary Movement (MRTA)

Date Formed 1983, with first terrorist acts in 1984.

Estimated Membership 100-200.

Headquarters Unknown.

Area of Operations Primarily in Lima, Peru.

Leadership Ernesto Montes Aliaga (AKA Raul Perez).

Other Names *Movimiento Revolucionario Tupac Amaru* (original language).

Sponsors Limited Nicaraguan and Cuban support suspected.

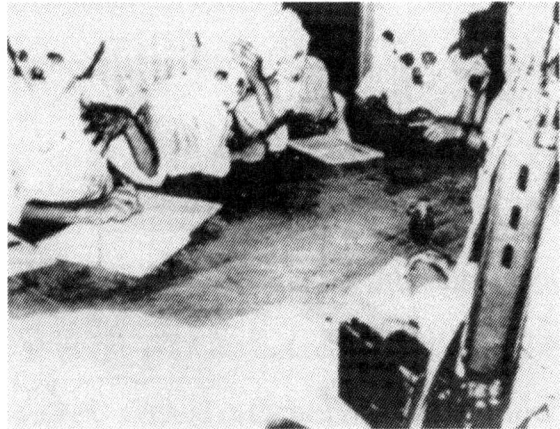

Armed members of the Tupac Amaru Revolutionary Movement posed for a news photo in Lima, Peru, in April 1985.

Political Objectives/Target Audiences
- Conduct "armed propaganda" to destabilize the Peruvian Government.
- Force US Government and business activities out of Peru.
- Create an image of MRTA as the Peruvian militant group aligned with Marxist international revolutionary movements and proponents, in contrast with the xenophobic *Sendero Luminoso* (SL) terrorist group.

Background

When the MRTA's name surfaced in 1984, many thought it was simply a front name for Peru's major terrorist/insurgent group, the SL. Available information indicates that the group is an independent organization formed by university student radicals who espouse a Castroite, Marxist-Leninist ideology.

Despite its short history, the MRTA has been very active. It has made attacks on US targets a definite policy. The tactics used and proficiency shown in MRTA attacks indicate a relatively high degree of skill.

Some contact apparently exists with other Latin American revolutionary groups, such as Colombia's 19th of April Movement (M-19). Some of the MRTA leadership lived in Cuba and the

111

Soviet Union in the 1970s after fleeing Peru during a Government crackdown on student radicals.

In fall 1986, the MRTA announced a merger with remnants of an earlier Peruvian radical group also referred to as the Movement of the Revolutionary Left (MIR). The group then conducted a series of bombings in Lima to publicize the new alliance.

A small organization, the MRTA requires relatively little money to support its operations. Through robberies and extortion activities directed at businessmen and narcotics traffickers, the MRTA appears capable of acquiring sufficient funds for its operations. Police raids have captured modern weapons, including automatic rifles and a wide variety of commercial and homemade explosives.

Selected Incident Chronology

March 1984 — Machinegunned the residence of a former Minister of Economy.

September 1984 — Killed a noncommissioned officer in a machinegun attack on a guard post at the Lima Naval Hospital.

October 1984 — Fired on the exterior of the US Embassy building.

March 1985 — Set fire to two Kentucky Fried Chicken restaurants and attempted to ignite a third.

July 1985 — Wounded three civilians in shooting and bomb attacks on six Lima police stations.

November 1985 — Bombed the Lima offices of Texaco Corporation.

November 1985 — Fired shots into the US Embassy compound and attempted to throw a bomb, which exploded on a sidewalk outside.

January 1986 — Occupied two radio stations and broadcast a protest of the visit of US Senator Kennedy.

April 1986 — Believed responsible for a car bomb at the US Ambassador's residence, as well as several other bombs at US and US-associated facilities, including banks and businesses.

August 1986 — Claimed responsibility for bombs placed in two Peruvian Government ministry buildings a few days after announcing an end to a self-proclaimed truce with the Garcia government.

September 1986 — Claimed an attack on the Chilean Embassy in solidarity with leftist groups opposing the Pinochet government in Chile.

December 1986 — Bombed with dynamite several US or US-associated facilities. Slogans painted on the buildings announced the merger of the MRTA and the MIR.

January 1987 — Ambushed and killed an Army recruiting officer in Huancayo.

January 1987 — Claimed credit for bombing a building housing offices of a US airline, the United Nations, and the Austrian Embassy.

February 1987 — Took over six radio stations in Lima to denounce the Government.

February-March 1987 — Conducted numerous bombings against branches of Peru's largest bank.

March 1987 — Took over a radio station, invaded a church, and occupied a private manufacturing concern to give revolutionary speeches and urge participation in the "armed struggle." This form of propagandizing was a new modus operandi for the MRTA-MIR groups.

March 1987 — Bombed with dynamite a container company. A manager who chased one terrorist was shot and killed by other terrorists during their escape.

April 1987 — Took over a radio station in Tacna and broadcast a 15-minute prerecorded message calling for armed struggle against the Garcia government.

May 1987 — Claimed responsibility for blowing up four buses in support of national work stoppage; again took over Lima radio stations to broadcast pro-MRTA propaganda.

June 1987 — Invaded two radio stations in Lima and forced them to broadcast a tape commemorating the second anniversary of a MRTA attack during the administration of President Belaunde.

June 1987 — Detonated a car bomb near the suburban Lima branch of Banco de Credito; MRTA propaganda was found at the scene.

August 1987 — Believed responsible for grenade attack against Presidential Palace.

September 1987 — By September had conducted some 39 bombings at major banking facilities in addition to bombings at Government offices, university sites, and US-owned business locations.

October 1987 — Set off small bombs at Bolivian Embassy and US Consulate annex.

November 1987 — Column of over 80 MRTA insurgents staged a carefully planned, well-publicized takeover of Juanjui, San Martin Province; departed area before security forces arrived.

February 1988 — Caused extensive damage but no injuries in bombings of Shell Oil offices, a pharmaceutical factory, a furniture store, and the Armco Peru plant in Lima.

March 1988 — Bombed the Lima headquarters of Anglo-Netherlands Royal Dutch Shell Oil Company, injuring two and causing considerable damage.

April 1988 — Simultaneously bombed two Lima US Information Service binational centers, damaging their facades and injuring two.

June 1988 — Fired three 60-mm mortar rounds at the residence of the US Ambassador. The attack caused minor damage.

Asian Terrorism

Terrorism in Asia has been on the rise since 1986. It occurs primarily as part of ongoing insurgencies, ethnic conflict, and domestic disputes, although in recent years Afghan-sponsored terrorism in Pakistan and Abu Nidal Organization activities in India and Pakistan demonstrate the ease of operations for states and transnational groups in Asia. Asian insurgent and dissident groups rarely seek out foreigners, however, directing their violence instead at domestic targets.

The use of terrorism by the two major insurgent groups in Asia — the Filipino Communists and the Sri Lankan Tamil guerrillas — differs markedly. The military wing of the Communist Party of the Philippines (CPP), the New People's Army (NPA), employs terrorism as a calculated and precise tactic to intimidate the population and eliminate key Government figures. NPA terrorism usually consists of assassinations carried out by hit teams called "sparrow" units. The CPP and NPA decision to target Americans, as in the killing of Clark Air Base personnel in October 1987, reflects careful calculation of political, strategic, and tactical benefits.

The Tamil separatist insurgents of Sri Lanka use terrorism as a widespread, often indiscriminate tactic. Lacking the rigid military organization of the NPA, the Tamils use terror in an uncalculated, crude, and often ineffective manner. Bombings, assassinations, and assaults against civilian targets are common, and the general population is increasingly at risk. The Tamils have conducted operations against foreigners infrequently, as in the May 1986 jetliner bombing in Colombo, which killed several Europeans.

In India, Sikh terrorism remains primarily domestic, but the Sikhs have demonstrated amply their ability to operate on an international scale. Sikh terrorist operations consist primarily of bombings, often against civilian targets, and assassinations of Government officials and moderate Sikhs. Sikh activity outside India was illustrated most dramatically by the 1985 bombing of an Air India flight over the North Atlantic. There has been, however, no comparable attack outside India since then.

Terrorism in Japan has continued at a generally low level, with the Chukaku-Ha, a radical leftist group, launching periodic incendiary and rocket attacks at Japanese and US facilities. The international terrorist group Japanese Red Army, responsible for the 1973 Lod airport massacre in Israel, has conducted terrorist operations in Europe and Asia as well as in the Middle East. The recent reemergence of this group after a hiatus of several years is particularly troublesome.

In Pakistan, the bloody September 1986 Abu Nidal Organization attempt to hijack a Pan Am airliner in Karachi highlighted the potential of transnational terrorism in Asia. Afghanistan's Ministry of State Security, WAD, has sponsored an increasingly violent terrorist bombing campaign in Pakistan, particularly in the Northwest Frontier Province. Over 200 Afghan refugees and Pakistani civilians have been killed and 1,200 wounded in over 100 attacks attributed to the WAD in 1987 alone.

North Korea practices terrorism on its own behalf against South Korea, as illustrated dramatically in November 1987 when two North Korean agents placed bombs aboard a Korean Air flight (KAL 858), causing the loss of the aircraft and all 115 passengers. Prior to that incident, North Korean terrorism had been directed principally against senior South Korean leaders, as evidenced in a 1983 bombing incident in Rangoon in which several South Korean Cabinet ministers died. North Korea also provided training to various international groups in the 1970s.

Iran and Libya have shown interest in Asia. They have attempted to recruit followers among lower class Muslims and have established basic infrastructures in the region.

Asian Incidents

Number of Incidents

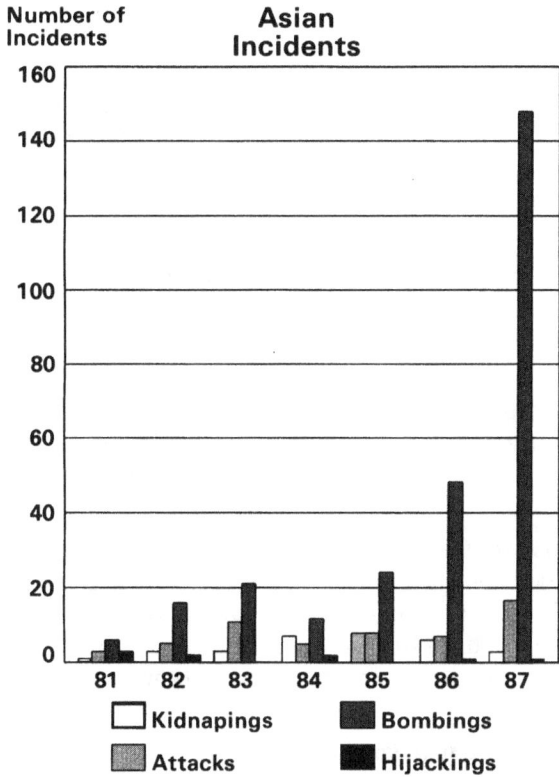

Kidnapings Bombings
Attacks Hijackings

Anti-US Attacks Asia

Number of Incidents

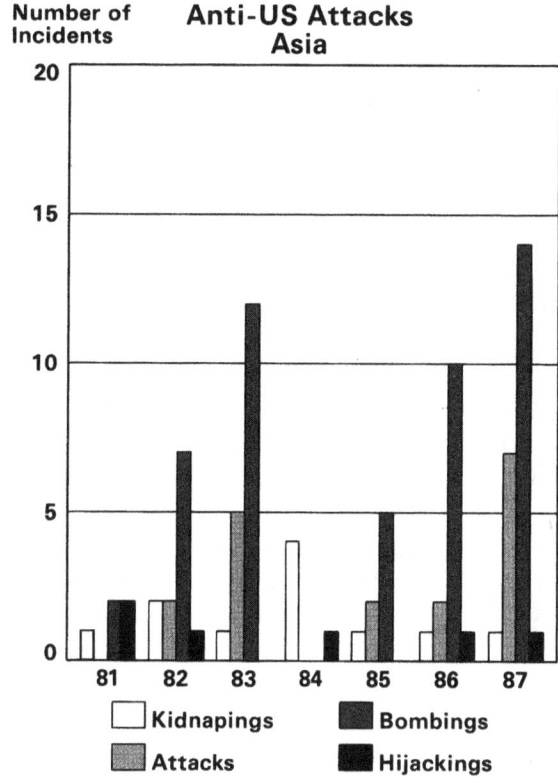

Kidnapings Bombings
Attacks Hijackings

Chukaku-Ha

Date Formed 1963.

Estimated Membership 3,000 (200 dedicated).

Headquarters Japan.

Leadership Takuji Mukai, Higeo Yamamori.

Other Names Middle Core or Nucleus Faction.

Sponsors Self-sustaining.

Political Objectives/Target Audiences
- Abolish the current constitutional democracy.
- Abolish the monarchy.
- Terminate the US-Japan Security Treaty and remove US forces from Japan.
- Halt construction of New Tokyo International Airport (NTIA).

Background

The Chukaku-Ha is the most powerful faction of the Japanese "New Left," or extreme leftwing radicals, which is composed of 23 factions. Official estimates of the strength of the New Left organizations are in the 35,000 range, including sympathizers.

The Chukaku-Ha developed after a confrontation and subsequent split from the Kakumaru-Ha, which had been the foremost organizer of the New Left until 1983. At issue between the two factions was whether to develop the philosophy of the New Left or to concentrate on instigating a mass struggle. The Chukaku-Ha opted for developing a mass struggle.

The Chukaku-Ha became the more active and adopted terrorism as a tactic. The operational and tactical skills of the group are imaginative and include use of timed incendiary devices, flamethrowers, and mortar-like launchers, often referred to as "rockets." Despite such technical proficiency, only a few injuries have resulted from Chukaku-Ha attacks.

The Chukaku-Ha operatives are a very secretive group, avoiding public gatherings or demonstrations. Contacts with outsiders are severely restricted.

The Chukaku-Ha focuses its attacks primarily upon Japanese Government buildings, construction of the NTIA, or upon the national railway system, although it has claimed responsibility for a number of attacks against US facilities. Public statements in the group periodical, *Zenshin* ("Advance"), indicate that specific individuals also could be targeted. This shift in tactics and continuing improvements in weapons technology are of growing concern to Government security organizations.

Funds for the group are generated from contributions solicited from the general membership to support the nearly 200 dedicated activists who have no other source of income.

A front-mounted flamethower truck of the type used by Chukaku-Ha in several bombing incidents since 1983. The device is set off by a terrorist in the vehicle, and a timed incendiary device is left behind to destroy the truck upon completion of the attack. This technique was used successfully against the Liberal Democratic Party Headquarters in Tokyo on 19 September 1984.

Selected Incident Chronology

June 1979 — Burned two vehicles and cut communications lines to Haneda airport in Tokyo when President Carter arrived.

September 1984 — Attacked the Liberal Democratic Party headquarters with a truck-mounted flamethrower and exploded a time bomb near the Israeli Embassy.

January 1985 — Used another truck-mounted flamethrower in an attack on the National Research Institute of Police Science, Tokyo.

April 1985 — Used a mortar-like weapon in simultaneous attacks on Narita and Haneda airports. No casualties, but major damage to at least one building.

November 1985 — Stormed and set ablaze several of Japan's busiest rail stations.

March 1986 — Launched projectiles at the Imperial Palace.

May 1986 — Launched projectiles at the buildings housing the Economic Summit. The improvised devices flew approximately 3,500 meters.

September 1986 — Reuter reported that unidentified attackers, suspected of being members of the Chukaku-Ha, battered a railway trade union official to death and badly wounded eight others in a series of attacks in their homes.

October 1986 — Police arrested seven suspected members of Chukaku-Ha and discovered a bomb factory in northern Japan.

November 1986 — Claimed responsibility for two timed incendiary devices that exploded at the residence of a former executive of the airport public corporation.

March 1987 — Claimed responsibility for a series of bombings intended to stop construction companies involved with expanding Narita airport.

July 1987 — Targeted vehicles owned by firms involved in constructing the new Kansai International Airport in Osaka and expanding Narita; used timed incendiary devices at 13 different locations on the same day.

August 1987 — Launched four incendiary devices from the bed of a stolen truck in the direction of the Imperial Palace. The truck went up in flames afterwards without causing any major damage or injuries.

January 1988 — Fired five rocket bombs toward the New Tokyo International Airport at Narita. The rockets were launched at the airport from a truck parked on an empty lot. No damage and no injuries were reported.

Japanese Red Army (JRA)

Date Formed 1971.

Estimated Membership 25.

Headquarters Lebanon.

Area of Operations Western Europe, Middle East, Asia.

Leadership Fusako Shigenobu (AKA Marian Fusako Okudaira, Miss Yuki), Haruo Wako.

Other Names *Nippon Sekigun, Nihon Sekigun.*

Sponsors Popular Front for the Liberation of Palestine, Libya.

Fusako Shigenobu, leader of the Japanese Red Army.

Political Objectives/Target Audiences
- Support the worldwide Marxist-Leninist revolution by conducting acts of terrorism.
- Serve as a uniting force for leftist anarchist organizations in Japan.
- Oppose Japanese imperialism.
- Establish a People's Republic in Japan.

Background

The Japanese Red Army (JRA) terrorist group was formed in 1971 by Fusako Shigenobu. While serving as liaison between the Japanese Red Army Faction and Palestinian terrorists, Shigenobu formed the JRA with a small cadre of personnel who had joined her in Lebanon. The core strength of the organization probably never exceeded 20-25, and a base of sympathizers in Japan probably numbered about 100. Homeland supporters provided some moral support and financial aid as well as an audience for JRA propaganda. The primary source of funds, however, is believed to be Palestinian factions and probably Libya.

The JRA conducted terrorist acts on behalf of the Popular Front for the Liberation of Palestine (PFLP) from 1972 to 1977, most notably the 1972 Lod Airport massacre in Israel. It also has acted independently over the years, although the JRA probably consults with the PFLP prior to conducting any attacks for its own purposes. JRA members who are still at large are believed to operate out of Lebanon with the PFLP.

Since 1977, the JRA has not claimed credit for violent actions; however, individuals formerly identified as members of the JRA have been linked individually to acts of terrorism as recently as 1988. Though JRA member Osamu Maruoka was arrested in Japan last November and suspected member Yu Kikumura (formerly with the Japanese Red Army Faction) was arrested in New Jersey in April 1988, the majority of JRA core members remain in Lebanon.

Selected Incident Chronology

May 1972 — Carried out a machinegun and grenade attack at Lod Airport. Three JRA members killed 26 people, including 16 Puerto Rican citizens on a pilgrimage to the Holy Land.

January-February 1974 — Attacked Shell Oil refinery storage tanks in Singapore and seized ferryboat crew and hostages. All hostages released unharmed.

September 1974 — Seized 11 hostages at the French Embassy in The Hague. The terrorists demanded, and were provided, an airliner for transport to Syria. Two Dutch police were wounded during the incident.

August 1975 — Ten members of the JRA took over the US Consulate in Kuala Lumpur, Malaysia, and seized 52 hostages, including the Consul and the Swedish Charge. The terrorists threatened to blow up the building and kill hostages unless seven JRA prisoners in Japan were released and allowed safe passage to the Middle East. Although the Japanese Government was willing to release the prisoners, only five were willing to go; they were flown to Tripoli, Libya, by way of Kuala Lumpur.

September-October 1977 — Hijacked a Japan Airlines plane in Bombay and forced it to land in Dhaka, Bangladesh. The Japanese Government agreed to release 9 imprisoned terrorists and to pay $6 million in exchange for 159 hostages. After payment of the ransom and the release of six JRA prisoners, the hijackers were flown to Algeria.

May 1986 — JRA member Yu Kikumura, 33, was arrested for having a bomb in his luggage at the Schiphol Airport in Amsterdam. He was later deported to Japan. Kikumura had been a member of the Black Helmet (Kuro Hero) radical organization in Japan before that group joined forces with the JRA in summer 1971.

June 1986 — Indonesian police released photographs of Tsutomu Shirosaki, 38, a JRA member whose fingerprints were found in a hotel room from which crude mortars were fired at the Japanese and US Embassy buildings in Jakarta. Shirosaki also is wanted for a car bombing outside the Canadian Embassy in Jakarta on May 14. The Anti-Imperialist International Brigades (AIIB) claimed responsibility.

June 1987 — Fired two rockets at the British Embassy in Rome. About 30 minutes later, detonated a car bomb across the street from the US Embassy. Within minutes, launched two homemade rockets at the US Embassy compound. Once again, the AIIB claimed responsibility, leading to the belief of JRA involvement.

November 1987 — Osamu Maruoka, a high-ranking JRA member, was arrested in Tokyo. Diverse travel throughout Asia and other evidence indicate he may have been attempting to establish a broader base in East Asia, possibly under the name of the Antiwar Democratic Front (ADF).

April 1988 — JRA member Yu Kikumura was arrested in New Jersey with three pipe bombs in his possession.

April 1988 — Planted a bomb in front of the US servicemen's club in Naples, Italy, killing five people, including a US servicewoman. Two JRA members are the main suspects in the bombing, which coincided with the anniversary of the US raid on Libya in 1986.

July 1988 — Attempted two rocket attacks, with makeshift launchers, against the US Embassy in Madrid, Spain. AIIB claimed responsibility.

NOTE: The JRA has not claimed any of these most recent attacks but is suspected of acting in the name of the Anti-Imperialist International Brigades (AIIB). The AIIB has carried out rocket attacks on US Embassies in Jakarta in 1986 and Madrid in 1988, as well as a coordinated bomb and rocket attack on the US Embassy in Rome in June 1987.

Liberation Tigers of Tamil Eelam (LTTE)

Date Formed 1972.

Estimated Membership 2,000 active.

Headquarters Jaffna Peninsula, Sri Lanka.

Area of Operations Sri Lanka.

Leadership Vellupillai Prabhakaran, leader; Anton Balasingam, spokesman.

Other Names Tigers, Tamil Tigers.

Sponsors Formerly by the Tamil Nadu State, India.

Political Objectives/Target Audiences
- Create a separate Tamil state in the northern and eastern provinces of Sri Lanka.
- Sabotage any negotiations between the governments of Sri Lanka and India and moderate Sri Lankan Tamils, leading to a negotiated settlement of the Sri Lankan conflict within the framework of a unitary Sri Lanka; force Indian troops to leave Sri Lanka.
- Eliminate moderate Tamils and other Tamil militant groups that compete with the LTTE for influence and power within the Sri Lankan Tamil community.
- Focus international attention on the plight of the Tamils living in Sri Lanka, concentrating especially on human rights issues.

Background

Long the strongest Sri Lankan Tamil militant group, the LTTE is the only major group that has fought the Indian Peacekeeping Force in Sri Lanka. The LTTE was formed in the early 1970s by young Sri Lankan Tamils who sought a separate Tamil state in Sri Lanka as a way of redressing Tamil grievances against the Sri Lankan Government. The LTTE gained notoriety after it claimed responsibility for the 1975 murder of Alfred Doriappa, the mayor of Jaffna.

The LTTE started its campaign for a separate Tamil state in earnest in 1977 with assassination attempts on several moderate Tamil politicians. Since the widespread communal riots of 1983, the LTTE has expanded its operations to include attacks on Sri Lankan security forces, bank robberies, and indiscriminate attacks on Sri Lankan officials and civilians in Sri Lanka's northern and eastern provinces. The LTTE also has fought with other, weaker Tamil militant groups in an attempt to ensure its preeminence. The LTTE has come under considerable pressure since October 1987, when the Indian Peacekeeping Force attacked and seized the LTTE stronghold of Jaffna city. This action was in response to continued LTTE attacks against civilians in the east and the LTTE's refusal to turn in its weapons and accept the accord. Since the seizure of Jaffna city, the Indian Peacekeeping Force has continued its actions against remaining LTTE fighters in the north and east.

Selected Incident Chronology

April 1975 — Claimed responsibility for the murder of Jaffna mayor Alfred Doriappa.

July 1983 — Ambushed and killed 13 soldiers, setting off islandwide ethnic riots.

April 1986 — Killed many members of another Tamil group (TELO) after a week of fighting.

May 1986 — Suspected of organizing the bombing of an Air Lanka aircraft at Colombo airport, killing 15.

June 1986 — Believed to be behind the placing of a rickshaw bomb in front of a crowded Colombo movie theater, and exploding time bombs on two buses.

July 1986 — Blamed for placing bombs on buses over a 3-day period, causing an estimated 100 deaths.

September 1986 — Murdered a German engineer attached to the Deutsche Welle radio-relay station.

December 1986 — In 1 week, attacked and killed over 90 members of a rival militant group, the Eelam People's Revolutionary Liberation Front.

February 1987 — Hacked to death 28 sleeping villagers, including 5 women and 10 children in Ampara, Sri Lanka.

April 1987 — Bombed central bus station in Colombo, killing 106 people and wounding 295 others.

April 1987 — Attacked 4 buses, killing 107 people near the village of Aluth-Oya.

June 1987 — Attacked a busload of Buddhist monks traveling south of Batticaloa, killing 29 and wounding 17.

October 1987 — When 12 captured LTTE members committed suicide by taking cyanide capsules, the group unleashed a wave of terrorist attacks in reprisal, killing more than 200, including several captured Sri Lankan soldiers.

May 1988 — Planted two landmines in Trincomalee; explosions killed seven members of the Indian Peacekeeping Force.

A body lies burning in the street in the outskirts of Colombo, Sri Lanka, after 5 days of rioting in July 1983. The riots were started after Tamil Tiger terrorists ambushed a patrol of Sinhalese Sri Lankan soldiers.

New People's Army (NPA)

Date Formed 1969.

Estimated Membership 20,000.

Headquarters Manila (National Democratic Front), central and northern Luzon (the underground Communist Party of the Philippines).

Leadership Rolando Kintanar (imprisoned) and Benito Tiamzon (probable chairman).

Sponsors Independent.

Political Objectives/Target Audiences
- Replace the current Aquino government with a Communist regime.
- Consolidate gains in the rural areas and focus on winning peasant support.
- Slowly erode support of the general Filipino populace for the continued US military presence on the islands.
- Provoke a more repressive response from the Aquino government through its counterinsurgency effort, thereby alienating larger segments of the Filipino populace.

Background

A Maoist-oriented insurgent organization, the NPA is the military wing of the Communist Party of the Philippines (CPP), a political organization formed in 1968. The CPP is dedicated to overthrowing the current Filipino regime by employing Maoist principles of peasant revolution, involving protracted guerrilla warfare. Since its inception, the NPA has increased steadily in size and capability; insurgent activities concomitantly have escalated in scope and magnitude. The group has been fairly successful in the rural areas of the country, where it has been able to exert influence and even establish control over village communities.

In the years following its inception, the NPA conducted rural insurgent operations throughout many of the country's provinces. Operations often were conducted on a local or regional level, usually with the intent of securing weapons and funds and harassing security forces. As it grew in size, strength, and confidence, the NPA increasingly became engaged in a campaign of intimidation and terror, as it began to target local and provinicial government officials opposed to the Communist movement. Other frequent targets included security personnel, local police units, informants, and members of the media who openly espoused anti-Communist rhetoric.

The Government's inability to curb the growth of the movement was not just a failed counterinsurgency effort. The Marcos regime also had failed to institute the necessary political, social, and economic reforms, as well as to curb rampant corruption, moves that would have placated critics and won back popular support. As they gained momentum, the CPP and the NPA were able to expand their influence into the urban areas of the nation. Their political strength also was enhanced through activities undertaken within the sphere of the groups' legal political organization, the National Democratic Front.

Except for an incident in which three US naval officers were killed near Subic Bay Naval Base in 1974, until fall 1987 the NPA had refrained from actively targeting Americans. The group has, however, conducted continuous surveillance and intelligence collection operations against US personnel and assets throughout the years. In recent years, the group had threatened to target any US personnel involved in either the counterinsurgency effort or the internal affairs of the Philippines. On 28 October 1987, however, two US servicemen and a retiree, in addition to a Filipino bystander, were assassinated in Angeles City. A spokesman for the National Democratic Front claimed responsibility for the attack on behalf of the NPA.

Selected Incident Chronology

April 1974 — Murdered three US naval personnel near Subic Bay Naval Base.

September 1978 — Assassinated the mayor of Kalinga Apayo.

February 1979 — Killed the son of then-Commanding General of the Philippine Army.

December 1981 — Implicated in kidnaping the son-in-law of President Marcos; the NPA denied involvement.

April 1982 — Assassinated the mayor of Calbayog City.

July 1982 — Implicated in murders of mayors of Rizal and Digos.

April 1983 — Killed police chief and five Filipino officers at a dance in Barangay Tiblawan.

November 1983 — Assassinated mayor of Luba.

May 1984 — Assassinated Brigader General Karnizal, police commander of Quezon City (claimed by the Alex Boncayao Brigade, an elite "sparrow unit" of the NPA).

September 1984 — Infiltrated a prison armory in Managna Abuyoz on Leyte Island, seizing an unspecified number of assorted weapons.

November 1984-January 1985 — Assassinated mayors of Zamboanga City and Santa Ana, the deputy mayor of Lapuyan, and police chief of Nueva Ecija.

September 1987 — CPP Party Chairman, Rudolpho Salas, arrested.

October 1987 — Murdered two American servicemen, an American retiree, and a Filipino bystander. Claimed by the Alex Boncayao Brigade, and later by the National Democratic Front on behalf of the NPA.

Sikh Terrorism

Background

Numerous Sikh terrorist organizations worldwide have been involved in a variety of violent activities. Nevertheless, information concerning the culpability of specific Sikh groups for specific operations or even on the infrastructures of Sikh elements is sparse. For these reasons, only two of the more notorious organizations are described in the profiles that follow: the Dal Khalsa and the Dashmesh Regiment.

A small, but violent movement emerged in 1981 when Sant Jarnail Singh Bhindranwale began preaching Sikh fundamentalism and urging the Sikh community in India to pressure the Government for an independent Sikh state. Bhindranwale's followers and supporters adopted terrorism as one of their tactics. In June 1984, Indian troops stormed the Golden Temple in Amritsar, Sikhism's holiest shrine, where Bhindranwale and his followers had made their headquarters. Bhindranwale and many followers were killed in the exchange. Sikh bodyguards of Prime Minister Indira Gandhi subsequently assassinated her.

Sikh advocates of a separate Sikh state of Khalistan since have engaged in bombings, sabotage, and indiscriminate murders of numerous Government officials and civilians in an effort to keep the Khalistani cause prominent. Funding for terrorist operations appears to be generated strictly from within the Sikh community in India and abroad.

Radical Sikhs have sought to escalate Hindu-Sikh tensions further by committing atrocities against Hindus throughout the Punjab and surrounding states. The radicals probably are hoping to provoke more violent Hindu reprisals against Sikh communities. Such an outcome would serve only to enhance the cause for Khalistan further by exacerbating communal animosities and weakening the stance of the moderates.

Selected Incident Chronology

October 1984 — Prime Minister Indira Gandhi's Sikh bodyguards assassinated her, purportedly for her ordering of the assault on the Golden Temple.

May 1986 — Attempted to shoot a Punjabi official visiting in Canada.

December 1986 — United Press International reported that more than 500 people, mostly Hindus, were killed by Sikh extremists across the Punjab in 1986.

April 1987 — Sikh extremists suspected by police of placing a 65-pound bomb in a crowded railway station in New Dehli, India; the bomb was discovered 90 minutes before it was set to explode.

July 1987 — Claimed responsibility for three separate attacks on bus passengers, in which 76 were killed and over 20 were wounded.

Dal Khalsa

Date Formed 13 April 1978.

Estimated Membership 200.

Headquarters Punjab.

Area of Operations India.

Leadership Gurbachan Singh Manochahal.

Other Names Unknown.

Sponsors Possibly Gurdev Singh, Arudh Singh, Dhana Singh, and Gurbachan Singh Manochahal.

Political Objectives/Target Audiences
- Create an independent Sikh state in the Punjab.
- Target the Indian Government, the Sikh moderate community, and Hindus in general.

Background

The Dal Khalsa, the oldest of the Sikh separatist groups, was established with the avowed object of demanding an independant sovereign Sikh state. It became involved in terrorism after the Sikh independence movement turned violent under Sant Jarnail Singh Bhindranwale in 1981. The Dal Khalsa was banned officially by the Indian Government after allegedly participating in the April 1982 Sikh-Hindu rioting. Manochahal is one of the most wanted Sikh extremists in the Punjab; there is a reward for his capture, dead or alive.

Selected Incident Chronology

September 1981 — Five members of the Dal Khalsa, armed with knives, seized an Indian Airlines plane between New Delhi and Srinagar and demanded freedom for Bhindranwale and $500,000 in cash for release of the aircraft.

August 1986 — Claimed responsibility for the assassination of General A. S. Vaidya, Chief of the Indian Army Staff, during the 1984 Army assault on the Golden Temple. Said that Vaidya had been on their "hit list" since the attack.

June 1987 — Murdered 12 people in 2 separate incidents in Udhwuk village.

Dashmesh Regiment

Date Formed Around 1982.

Estimated Membership About 200 members.

Headquarters Central headquarters probably located in the Punjab.

Area of Operations Throughout India, especially in Punjab and Haryana, and to some extent worldwide.

Leadership Unknown.

Other Names None known.

Sponsors Various Sikh leaders.

Political Objectives/Target Audiences
- Establish Khalistan as an autonomous Sikh state.
- Target Indian Government officials, moderate Sikhs, and Hindu residents of the Punjab.

Background

The Dashmesh "Tenth" Regiment probably was organized under the aegis of Sant Jarnail Singh Bhindranwale. After conducting a reign of terror in the Punjab in the early 1980s, he was killed by the Indian Army in a June 1984 attack on the Sikh Golden Temple. The group was named after the Sikhs' revered 10th and last guru, Gobind Singh, who in the 18th century, in addition to greatly influencing the Sikh religion, forged the Sikhs into a warrior class.

The Dashmesh Regiment's founder is reputed to have been Major General Shaheg Singh, a Sikh officer with experience training irregulars in Bangladesh, who subsequently was cashiered from the Indian Army for corruption. However, shortly before his death in the attack on the Golden Temple, the general vehemently disclaimed any connection with the Dashmesh Regiment or any knowledge about such a regiment. Surinder Singh Gill, an orthodox Sikh who gave up a prized civil service position to join Bhindranwale, probably was the group's first leader. Following the assault on the Golden Temple, Dashmesh gained increased covert and popular support and has continued to claim responsibility for terrorist attacks throughout India.

Selected Incident Chronology

March 1984 — Claimed credit for shooting and killing Singh Manchandi, president of the management committee of the main Sikh temple in New Delhi.

April 1984 — Claimed credit for shooting and killing V. N. Tiwari, a rightwing Hindu politician and identified pro-Government member of Parliament.

April 1984 — Sent a letter to the *Indian Express* (India's third largest newspaper) threatening to assassinate Prime Minister Indira Gandhi.

April 1984 — In a coordinated series of arson incidents, set fire to 37 railroad stations in Punjab and sabotaged railroad lines and communications facilities.

May 1984 — Claimed credit for shooting to death Ramesh Chander, editor in chief of the *Hind Samacher* (India News) in Jullundur, Punjab.

November 1984 — A caller who identified himself as a member of the Dashmesh Regiment made a telephone threat to assassinate world leaders converging on New Delhi for the funeral of Mrs. Indira Gandhi; he stated that dignitaries from the Soviet Union, Vietnam, and the Palestine Liberation Organization were on the Dashmesh death list.

June 1985 — Claimed credit for an incident at Tokyo's Narita International Airport when a bomb destined for placement on an Air India jumbo jet exploded prematurely, killing two baggage handlers. Also claimed credit for the midair destruction of a second Air India jumbo jet from a bomb in the luggage compartment; the aircraft was lost off the coast of Ireland, killing all passengers. Another terrorist group, the Kashmir Liberation Army, also claimed responsibility for the two incidents.

December 1985 — Claimed credit for shooting and killing Hindu physician, Dr. Anil Baghi, in Ferozepur, Punjab; the Dashmesh Regiment said Baghi had been punished for the anti-Sikh writings of his father, a journalist.

April 1986 — Killed a senior leader of Prime Minister Rajiv Gandhi's Congress party.

October 1986 — Attempted to assassinate Prime Minster Rajiv Gandhi during a ceremory at Mahatma Gandhi's tomb.

African Terrorism

International terrorism in Africa generally presents a low level of threat. The greatest hazards to US citizens from terrorism are from individuals or groups sponsored by Libya's intelligence organization, from the Abu Nidal Organization, and from accidental involvement in domestic terrorist activity by insurgents against their own governments. The level of domestic terrorist violence by indige-

nous insurgent groups, however, can be very high. For example, in Mozambique, the National Resistance of Mozambique (RENAMO) has employed large-scale violence against noncombatant civilian populations in an apparently coordinated pattern. Over 100,000 civilians are estimated to have been killed in 1986-88.

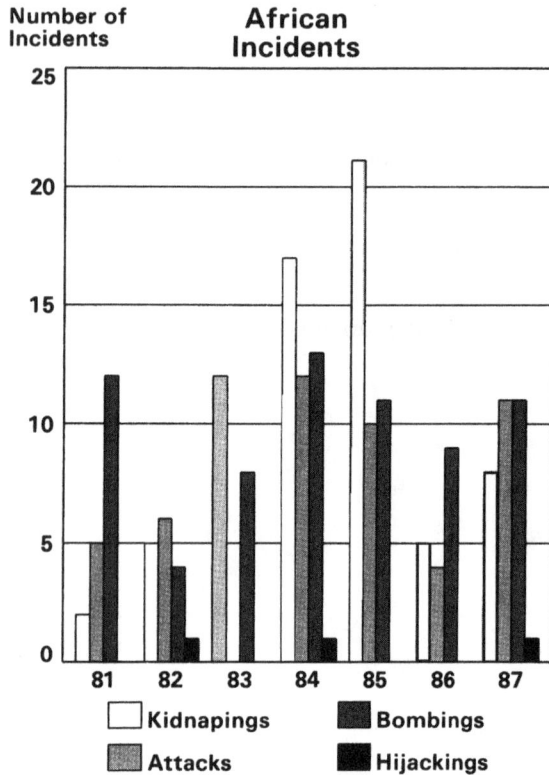

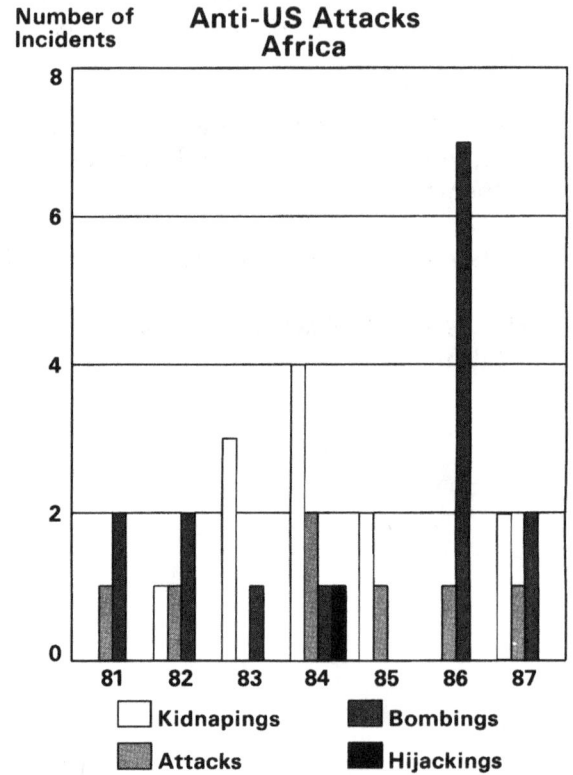

Number of Incidents

African Incidents

Kidnapings   Bombings
Attacks   Hijackings

Number of Incidents

Anti-US Attacks Africa

Kidnapings   Bombings
Attacks   Hijackings

African National Congress (ANC)

Date Formed In 1912 as the South African Native National Congress; in 1923 renamed African National Congress.

Estimated Membership 4,000 to 5,000.

Headquarters Lusaka, Zambia.

Area of Operations South Africa (bases in Zambia and Angola, and cells in other "front line" states).

Leadership Oliver Tambo (acting president), Nelson Mandela (imprisoned since 1962).

Other Names *Umkhonto We Sizwe* (Spear of the Nation) is the military or operational wing of the ANC.

Sponsors Receives support from the Soviet Bloc, Cuba, and a number of African nations, in addition to contributions from the West.

Political Objectives/Target Audiences
- Overthrow the current South African regime and dismantle the system of apartheid.
- Establish a multiracial Socialist government in South Africa.
- Secure the release of Nelson Mandela and other ANC members held in South African prisons.
- Isolate the present South African regime in world opinion.

Background

In 1910, by an act of British Parliament, the newly established Union of South Africa became a dominion of the British Empire. Reacting to legislation and a constitution that virtually guaranteed white dominance, a group of black lawyers held a conference in Bloemfontein in 1912, from which was born the South African Native National Congress. The name was changed to the African National Congress in 1923.

The ANC functioned principally as a forum to express black African opinion, wherein protests against discriminatory practices could be voiced and other means of peaceful protest used against apartheid. A decisive turning point occurred with the incident at Sharpeville in March 1960, when police fired upon demonstrators. Shortly thereafter the Government outlawed the ANC and arrested many of its members.

The ANC decided in 1961 that violence would be the only tool that could force the South African Government to negotiate, and formed a military operations wing, the *Umkhonto We Sizwe* (MK). During the next 15 years, the MK conducted limited sabotage operations, with transportation and communications facilities the primary targets.

The ANC's bombing attacks intensified in 1980, beginning with the bombing of the South African Coal, Gas, and Oil Conversion Corporation (SASOL). In 1983, ANC operations — which heretofore had sought to avoid civilian casualties — abruptly changed. Attacks became more indiscriminate, resulting in both black and white civilian victims.

Although ANC operations have not posed any direct threat to US assets or personnel in South Africa, the indiscriminate nature of recent attacks raises the danger of Americans becoming inadvertent victims. In addition, in June 1986, ANC acting President Tambo issued a warning to all foreign firms operating in the country that their continued presence could be an indicator of their home governments' support for the South African regime; as such, they could become targets.

ANC personnel receive the majority of their training at camps in Angola. Some have received educational training in Tanzania. The group operates throughout all of the countries bordering South Africa, as it seeks to infiltrate South Africa to conduct various types of operations. The ANC receives many of its weapons from the Soviet Bloc.

Selected Incident Chronology

June 1980 — Attacked SASOL, resulting in $7 million in damage to fuel storage tanks.

December 1982 — Bombed the incomplete Koeberg nuclear powerplant outside of Cape Town.

May 1983 — Staged a car bombing of the South African Air Force Headquarters in Pretoria, killing 19 people and wounding 200.

May 1984 — Conducted a rocket attack on the Mobile Oil Refinery, causing several million dollars in damage.

December 1985 — Bombed shopping center near Durban, killing five whites.

June 1986 — Conducted two car bomb attacks in Johannesburg, killing several people and injuring many others.

October 1987 — Staged a car bombing in Durban, injuring five people. Botswana blamed the South African Government for this car bombing.

May 1987 — Exploded bombs near a downtown Johannesburg courthouse, killing four white policemen.

July 1987 — Exploded a car bomb outside the Witwaterstand Military Command Headquarters in central Johannesburg, injuring 68.

April 1988 — Exploded three bombs in Pretoria, damaging a theater near the Holiday Inn. One person was killed, reportedly the ANC member who was planting one of the devices.

June 1988 — Exploded a bomb in Roodeport outside a Standard bank office, killing four and injuring more than 19. The device, probably a limpet mine, was planted in a garbage can or flower box outside the bank.

June 1988 — Exploded a bomb at an art gallery in Johannesburg, killing one alleged ANC member (the suspected perpetrator).

July 1988 — Exploded a car bomb in Johannesburg outside of Ellis Park sports stadium, killing 2 and injuring 35 others. The bomb, 60-100 kilograms of explosives, was timed to go off as thousands of people were departing a rugby match.

Outlook

Terrorism is used now by a range of groups, insurgency movements, and states for carefully defined purposes. Anticipating a terrorist's intention to attack US citizens or facilities is a most difficult task. Today there are over 700,000 US Government military and civilian personnel, in addition to their approximately 400,000 dependents, stationed overseas. The greatest chance for successfully defending US lives and property lies in cooperative diplomatic, police enforcement, military, and intelligence efforts, as well as a national commitment to defeat terrorism and not to give in to terrorist demands.